MANAGE YOU!

Learn the Skills You Need to Grow as a Person and a Manager

M. J. Pontus

M. J. Pontus

© Copyright 2022 M. J. Pontus, Malu Me Limited

All rights reserved.

This book's contents may not be reproduced, duplicated, or transmitted without the author's direct written permission.

Under no circumstances will any legal responsibility or blame be held against the publisher for any reparation, damages, or monetary loss due to the information herein, either directly or indirectly.

Legal Notice:

This book is copyright protected. This is only for personal use. You cannot amend, distribute, sell, use, quote or paraphrase any part of this book's content without the author's consent.

Disclaimer Notice:

Please note that the information contained within this document is for educational and entertainment purposes only. Every attempt has been made to provide accurate, up-to-date, reliable, and complete information. No warranties of any kind are expressed or implied. Readers acknowledge the author is not rendering legal, financial, medical or professional advice. The content of this book has been derived from various sources. Please consult a licensed professional before attempting any techniques outlined in this book.

By reading this document, the reader agrees under no circumstances is the author responsible for any direct or indirect losses incurred as a result of the use of the information contained within this document, including, but not limited to, errors, omissions, or inaccuracies.

ISBN: 978-1-7397389-8-3

TABLE OF CONTENTS

Introduction	1
Part A – It Starts with You - Self-Management Skills	3
Chapter 1: Organisation	17
Chapter 2: Goal Setting	27
Chapter 3: Time Management	35
Chapter 4: Self-Motivation	43
Chapter 5: Stress Management	51
Chapter 6: Decision Making	59
Chapter 7: Accountability	67
Chapter 8: Confidence	71
Chapter 9: Problem-Solving	81
Chapter 10: Meaningful Productivity	87
Chapter 11: Adaptability	93
Chapter 12: Conscientiousness	99

Chapter 13: Develop Self-Management Skills	105
Part B – All About Time Management	**113**
Chapter 14: Time Management Challenges	121
Chapter 15: Steps for Better Time Management	133
Part C – Life-Work Balance	**167**
Chapter 16: Redefine Work-Life Balance	169
Chapter 17: Managing Your Free Time	179
Chapter 18: Deal With Changes	183
Chapter 19: Learning to Say No!	189
Chapter 20: Focus on Self-Care	195
Chapter 21: Meaningful Relationships	205
Chapter 22: Preventing Burnout	211
Conclusion	**231**
References	**233**

M. J. Pontus

INTRODUCTION

Three decades ago, it was a common belief that everything you are and everything you can or cannot do was determined by a piece of paper called a diploma. What are your exam scores? How well did you perform in college? Did you even go to college? How about university? And even though everyone knew that education alone was not the only metric for how successful a person will be, a lot of weight rode on it.

Skills, on the other hand, were deemed an on-the-job learning opportunity. Sure, they were important, and if you had them, you stood out. But they always took a back seat.

Over the years, however, people have understood just how important these skills have become. How well you manage your time and set SMART goals, what it takes to be a productive member of society. How you manage yourself and the world around you and whether you're dynamic enough to embrace change have all become stipends of a successful individual's growth.

In short, skills are essential. And if you're in a management position, these skills are a must!

In this book, you will be introduced to some of the most basic, life-altering skills you will need to change how you view and interact with the world. You will learn all about managing your personal life, whether it's stress, problem-solving or just finding the motivation to keep going. You'll learn how to organise yourself and the world around you to reap the benefits of being a "whole" person who can differentiate between what's important and what's not without anxiety. You'll learn how to set SMART goals and the skills needed to follow through. You'll master time management and the different theories and practicalities that come with taking control of every minute of your day.

You'll come out a different person and be the better for it.

So let's dive in, shall we?

PART A: IT STARTS WITH YOU: SELF-MANAGEMENT

M. J. Pontus

Self-management skills do not just improve your performance at work but also bolster your productivity and efficiency. They are tools to help you achieve your professional goals and improve your chances of employability, offering control over the career path you have pursued. As a manager, developing these skills will showcase how dependable you are.

So, what are self-management skills? They are the self-regulating skills a person needs to control emotions, behaviours, and thoughts. They ensure you can efficiently deal with any situation. Managers with strong self-management skills establish not only independent goals for themselves, but they do everything required to achieve them as well. By developing new skills, you can appreciate and understand the importance of regulating your emotions and behaviour in the workplace. Any potential employer will tell you they want candidates with strong self-management skills because they can regulate their thoughts and emotions, which means they are more in control of themselves and the situation. You can take smarter actions to achieve your professional and career goals by regulating your behaviour.

Before you learn about the different self-management skills and how to develop them, understanding their importance is paramount. Knowing the benefits associated with any change you are trying to implement in your life is crucial. The benefits themselves act as a motivation for you to make the change sustainable. Developing self-management skills will improve your organisational skills and confidence and enhance your sense of accountability and responsibility. It will give you the strength and abilities to deal with any challenge that arises in the workplace. In addition, these skills enable you to set goals and prioritise to achieve the best possible results. In this opening chapter, you will be introduced to various self-management skills any successful manager must develop.

Organisation

The ability to stay organised is the backbone of self-management skills. But why? The answer to this lies in how the brain functions. The human brain is an incredibly complex organ - the most powerful one. It is the motor of our creativity, thinking, memory, problem-solving abilities, and much more. The brain is better equipped to think than to store. You might remember something that you did years ago but, struggle to recollect what you wore to work the other day. This is normal and has to do with short- vs long-term memory.

By offloading the storage function of the brain to an external system, staying organised becomes easy. An efficient organisation system gives you a means to not just capture ideas but also make a note of all the things you need to do. It will help keep track of all your tasks. Additionally, an organisation system will help store and retrieve information as needed. When you are organised, your overall efficiency will improve. Once you learn how to become organised, you are less likely to forget an important meeting or let things slip through the cracks. Over time, all the information, data, and notes gathered can gain helpful insights for reflection, analysis, and improvement. A combination of these factors will improve your efficiency as a manager.

Creating an effective organisational system isn't as daunting as it seems. You need to consider first the nature of the task at hand, which will allow you to carry it out in the best way possible. It's also essential to distinguish between important and urgent tasks to prioritise your workload and complete your day's or week's work. We will explore this in greater detail later.

Goal Setting

The second aspect of improving workplace productivity for all managers revolves around goal setting. Goals are essential objectives you wish to achieve, and only when a concrete plan of action supports a dream does it become a goal. A constant debate in the world of productivity is whether goals or systems are better. Some believe that goals are pointless without a system that enables us to achieve them. You cannot run a marathon by simply setting a goal. Instead, you will need to train daily, sign up for one, and then run the marathon.

For this reason, you need a combination of targets and systems to get where you want. A goal is your compass, showing the right direction. And the system enables you to move forward toward the goal you have established.

A goal is not just a random thought or a vague idea that pops into your head. It's not just something you find appealing or exciting. It is a destination, but it doesn't become a goal unless it has some personal meaning or value. Any goal you establish must be meaningful to you, measurable, attainable, and, most of all, have some kind of deadline.

Chances are, without combining these aspects, you are merely setting yourself up for failure.

The reason most people fail to meet their goals has to do with a lack of vision. What are you trying to accomplish? How will you feel once you've achieved a particular goal, and by contrast, what will it cost you if you cannot achieve it? These are all important considerations you must remember to optimise your goal-setting.

Time Management

A precious non-renewable resource most people take for granted is time. We all have a fixed number of hours at our disposal every day. However, only a few are successful when it comes to spending them wisely. The difference lies in the ability to manage the time available. Unless you learn to manage your time wisely, you cannot make the most of your life or any opportunity that comes your way. Mastering the art of time management is a crucial self-management skill, and it takes a great deal of dedication. As with any other skill, it is never too late to learn.

The first thing to understand about time management is that your time is your own. You do not owe it to anyone else. When you say that you don't have time for something, it just means the task is not a priority at the moment. Don't make the mistake of thinking you are doing things that others won't. Regardless of who is asking you to do it, you are ultimately the one doing it. Therefore, your time is within your control. It starts with learning to prioritise what you want to do and where you want to concentrate on the bulk of your efforts. When it comes to time management, you need to identify which task is important or urgent and prioritise it. It should add value to your life in some form. Whether it's a personal or professional goal, you cannot work on it without time.

Self-Motivation

There are times when you have something to do but just don't feel like doing it. Or perhaps you were excited to start a project only to realise that it would drain your energy. Both instances illustrate a lack of motivation. Self-motivation is an internal force or strength that pushes you to move ahead. It's the desire to develop, produce, achieve, and move forward in life. There will be instances when you want to quit something or don't even know how to get started with it. Or perhaps you are facing an obstacle that makes you want to give up altogether. No matter the situation, self-motivation is the fuel that propels you ahead and limits the urge to quit. It ensures that all your efforts until now come to fruition. One of the crucial aspects of a manager's job description is to motivate their employees and teams. That being said, you cannot inspire others if you are not motivated yourself.

Generally speaking, the key to self-motivation is to adopt healthy and sustainable habits and eliminate distractions. These not only drain your brain power, but they can also cause procrastination. Sharpening your focus is important in enabling you to find the motivation to pursue your goals and achieve whatever it is you want to achieve professionally.

Stress Management

Stress has become a staple of the modern lifestyle. If you want to lead a happy and satisfying life, you must ensure that stress does not get in the way. Not only is it a joy killer, but excessive stress and the inability to cope with it can hinder your sense of wellbeing. It can eat away your productivity and leave you unable to carry out even the most routine tasks.

We commonly toss the word stress around in regular conversations. Unfortunately, few understand what it really is. Stress is an internal reaction triggered by your body when it feels it is under threat. This stress can be physical and psychological. For instance, the nervousness you experience right before a big presentation is a response to the stress the situation is causing. The thought of not meeting a deadline can also cause stress, and this would be the same trigger response if a wild animal started chasing you.

Stress is one of the most overwhelming feelings anyone can experience. When left unregulated, it can precipitate the onset of physical health disorders and mental conditions. If you don't want to put your health at risk, then learning to tackle stress is critical. Stress management is bound to come in handy in your personal and professional life. In the end, when you can manage your stress effectively and efficiently, your wellbeing and ability to be productive improve.

Decision Making

We all make decisions every day. Some of them are minor, while others have significant impacts on our lives. Deciding something as simple as what to eat for dinner, where to go on holiday, or even the route you take to work are all decisions you make. Some major decisions include making a career change, accepting a promotion, and even moving. Because every decision produces its own effects, whether big or small, learning how to decide is a pillar of effective management.

As a manager, your decision-making skills are vital. That's because they not only influence what you do, but have great bearings on your team and their performance. You need to have faith in your decisions and show confidence. To make good decisions, you need to get rid of emotional attachment, be fair and unbiased, and avoid conflicts of interest. You must base your decisions on facts, sound logic, and reasoning, with a little touch of analysis. Others can weigh in, but, in the end, the decision must be yours to make. There will be different situations where the thought of deciding makes your head spin, throwing your management skills into question. All decisions are associated with low to high risk. However, once you go through the suggestions about decision-making given in the latter part of this book, your overall productivity as a manager will reach new heights.

Accountability

Many of us will look for a scapegoat whenever things don't go as planned. However, this is not a great attribute for a manager. Managers need accountability, not just toward their team, but themselves as well. Accountability refers to your capacity to take ownership of your thoughts, actions, and behaviours. Once you learn to become accountable, you can stop blaming others for your mistakes. It also allows you to learn to trust yourself. A combination of these factors will make you a better decision-maker overall. When you hold yourself accountable to someone or something, it helps build trust. It also ensures that you are committed to doing the right thing, regardless of how tough the circumstances get.

It goes without saying that no one wants a colleague or manager who doesn't take responsibility or own up to their mistakes. Rather than place the blame on a co-worker or a client's seemingly unrealisable demands, aspiring managers must take it upon themselves to be accountable and keep the flow of work going. In doing so, you are boosting your productivity and setting an excellent example for others to follow.

Confidence

A core character trait that attracts us to others is confidence. Some seem to effortlessly ooze confidence, while others are nervous wrecks most of the time. A confident manager is someone who commands the trust of their team and other employees. You cannot exhibit confidence unless you respect and trust your abilities. This enables you to step into a naturally positive role. Remember, positivity is contagious. It will eventually rub off on your employees, and the result will be highly productive and performing teams. Your collaborators will also be happier and more satisfied.

Learning to be confident is possible; the good news is that you don't have to be born with confidence. Instead, you can become more confident with effort, patience, and commitment. The first step in doing so is to detach yourself from what people think or say about you. Our lack of self-confidence often stems from our fear of being judged by others. When you learn to let go of people's opinions of you, you will project more confidence, and others will want to trust you. It will also make you a more self-assured and reliable person.

Problem-Solving

If everything always went according to plan, we would all achieve our goals in a heartbeat. Unfortunately, this isn't how life works. There will be different challenges, problems, and obstacles for you to face. Whether it is your personal or professional life, problems are a part of the human experience. Unless we learn how to deal with them and rise to the situation, we cannot hope to overcome them. Also, problems are not the end of the road. Rather, they are a learning opportunity to do things differently. Therefore, an important skill that all managers must develop is the ability to solve problems. Whether this involves dealing with a reluctant supplier or mediating a dispute between employees, great managers must be diplomats and quick thinkers. In the end, it isn't just the employees working under you who expect you to problem solve; your superiors will also have this expectation of you as a manager.

Problem-solving isn't just about dealing with the circumstances when they crop up. Instead, you need to get to the root of the problem. By assuming a fair and unbiased stance, you must analyse a tricky situation and find a desirable solution. The issues can be technical, or they can involve interpersonal skills. Regardless of what it is, learning how to solve the problem is paramount. You must be objective when it comes to problem-solving. With that, you need to identify the problem, its causes, and how to resolve it. Including the interested parties as much as possible will also contribute to appeasing tense situations and restoring peace.

Along with all this, you will need to find different solutions that stop the problem from reoccurring. No matter how bad the situation is, a manager must be fearless, think on their feet, and be diplomatic, which is what problem-solving is all about.

Meaningful Productivity

Nowadays, the phrase "I am busy" seems to be thrown around. However, staying busy is not the same as being productive. These are two completely different things. Productivity is also of different types. There's something known as meaningful productivity, which refers to the ability to focus on tasks that add significant value. For instance, you might have ten things that you need to accomplish within a given day. However, not all of them are of the same value. Some will be important and meaningful, while others are simple routine tasks that have to be completed. To become an excellent manager and improve your overall efficiency, you must focus on meaningful productivity - combining organisation, time management, and decision-making. Meaningful productivity fosters a sense of satisfaction and motivates you to keep going.

Adaptability

Since change is the only constant in life, learning to adapt is vital. Adaptability is your ability to learn new skills, get accustomed to changing rules and circumstances, learn new procedures and implement them, and improve your behaviour in response to any changes within the workplace. If you are not adaptable to change, you will not move ahead in life. Because change is also a requisite for growth and development, adaptability is a skill managers cannot do without. It promotes productivity and shows how resourceful you are. Adaptable managers are flexible and can respond to any external changes with great efficiency. They do not get derailed even when things do not go as planned. Instead, good managers can think quickly on their feet and adapt their thinking, behaviours, and actions to fit the new circumstances. Adaptability helps them keep the flow of work going without being overwhelmed by new rules, methods, or policies. This is a crucial leadership skill; once you learn to be adaptable, your ability to face challenges improves substantially.

Conscientiousness

Finally, you'll need to be more conscientious if you want to become an exceptional manager. Conscientiousness refers to the personality trait of being diligent and careful. It's an inherent desire to ensure that you perform all the tasks well and not leave anything to chance. Instead of being disorderly and easy-going, conscientiousness guarantees that you are efficient and well-organised at all times. It also gives you the strength to work through complex tasks or activities. Along with that, it creates a better sense of connectedness between you and your peers. A conscientious manager is ambitious, thoughtful, and dependable. They are excellent planners and gravitate toward leadership positions in any workplace.

CHAPTER 1: ORGANISATION

If you want to be an excellent manager, being organised is paramount, and there are two important reasons for it. When you are organised as a manager, your ability to focus on meaningful things increases, ensuring you are carrying them out properly. At the same time, it helps eliminate wasteful tasks and activities. If you are not organised, you cannot lead a high-performing team. You cannot expect them to be organised and deliver satisfactory results when you do not adhere to the same standard. As mentioned, an important aspect of effective management is to lead by example, or else others will not follow.

Unless you are highly organised as a manager, you cannot coach others to organise themselves better. This also optimises the performance of every individual in the organisation. Along with all these benefits, people thrive and work better in structured environments. If staying organised is something you typically struggle with or believe there is room for improvement, use the suggestions in this chapter to your advantage. You can do meaningful work, get ahead in your career, and be a better manager for your team once you learn to become and stay organised. This is an essential requisite for achieving a sustainable work-life balance. By reading this chapter, you will gain a better and deeper understanding of why an organisation matters in all your work endeavours and how to be and stay organised.

Focus on Important Work

You have multiple activities and tasks to complete every single day. In fact, there will rarely be a day when you have little to do. One thing you need to do is to learn to divide them and work them into different categories. Tasks are not equally important. Likewise, everyone doesn't create the same value or hold the same urgency. Divide the tasks at work into urgent and important categories. To become a highly organised manager, your primary focus should be at the top of your list. Even if something is marked urgent but barely adds or creates any value, stop wasting your time on it. Any task that doesn't make a real contribution is not important. These are often labelled as urgent, whether it is responding to emails, drafting reports, or attending meetings. However, you should understand that dedicating too much time to these can seriously waste your time and effort.

So, what are important tasks? Anything that creates value, delivers, or captures it for the organisation and other stakeholders qualifies as important. Consider your organisation's work philosophy and culture to determine whether a task is important or urgent. Focus on your personal goals, team goals, and organisational goals, and look for activities that directly or indirectly result in value creation. For instance, creating value in the business environment involves the building and maintaining strategic partnerships, creating and developing innovative products, and effective planning.

Similarly, being an inspiring coach, staying productive, and fostering an inclusive team environment are equally important responsibilities for a manager. For that reason, you must utilise your skill set to guarantee that your priorities are conducive to value creation, whether it's getting a project done early or landing a new big client. The better grasp you have on what needs to be accomplished, the better you will manage your time and that of your team.

Determine Real Progress

Some tasks are required for progress. For instance, a proper action plan cannot be devised without thorough research and analysis. Now, specific tasks might appear to be strongly associated with the goals you wish to achieve, but in reality, they don't amount to any concrete progress. You aren't making actual progress if you spend all the time available for planning or researching. So, unless you implement it, you cannot determine whether or not the plan is any good.

Similarly, having too many meetings reaching no conclusion is equally wasteful. This happens because it is easier to do certain things than to get started. Even if you aim to get only half of it done, the chances of doing it 100% are relatively good, after which you can adjust the course of action according to the feedback you receive. On the other hand, if you try to go overboard and aim for 100% results, especially while using overly complex or broad solutions, the plan will probably not work.

So, focus on making genuine progress instead of over-reading, over-analysing, overthinking and making matters too complicated. Rather than getting carried away with myriad tasks, identify what completed work means and then focus on all deliverables. It also helps to keep track of everything you and your team achieve within a given timeframe so you can recreate that dynamic for even greater progress in the future.

Delete, Delegate, and Do

Start following the concept of "delete, delegate, and do" if you want to stay organised. These three things can be done with any task you have to complete. Tending to urgent tasks feels good but can result in fake progress. Instead, direct all your time, attention, resources, and energy to meaningful activities that bring value. Develop the habit of eliminating unhelpful activities to improve your overall efficiency. The first part of this approach is to "do" or complete tasks. Focus on completing important tasks instead of those that result in no value creation. After this, the next step is delegation. Delegation refers to the decentralisation of authority so that others can do things. If there is a specific task, you know other team members can carry out successfully, delegate it to them. Once you delegate, it's imperative that you avoid micromanaging, which can make everyone's life at work downright miserable. Simply let them do their job. Don't get in their way unless they come to you asking for help or suggestions. Even if you view yourself as an expert or the only one who can do the job properly, eventually, it will result in complete burnout.

To become an organised manager and lead a highly productive team, you need to delegate tasks. This is how others will learn from you as well. You can also refocus your time, attention, energy, and resources toward more productive tasks once everything else is delegated.

The last aspect of this three-pronged approach is "delete." Any task that is not important and doesn't have to be or cannot be delegated to others should be deleted. There is no point in wasting precious resources on tasks that are neither important nor result in creating any value.

Time Tracking

If you want to stay organised, it's important that you keep track of your time and have control over it. Most people end up wasting precious hours without even knowing it. Even if they believe they are in charge of their time, they are not. One seemingly simple task may take them hours to complete, and they will get behind on work that truly matters. As you can imagine, this is by no means a sustainable way to organise your time at work. So, to become an organised manager, you should not only maintain control over your time but also track how it is utilised. To that end, you can use a journal or a time-tracking application. It will show where and how most of your time is dedicated and how much of it is misused. It involves analysing the areas where there is room for improvement, opportunities for growth, and areas in which you are lagging. If you are honest with yourself and deal with this metric, you can improve your team's and your own overall efficiency. Remember that at the end of the day, you cannot manage something that cannot be measured. As we'll see in the following chapter, the ability to measure your performance on the job and keep track of it is an essential component of your professional success.

Deal with Work Limitations

You don't imagine an overworked, stressed, or exhausted individual when you think of an organised person, do you? In reality, this happens when you don't limit yourself and your team in terms of work goals and workload. Organised managers must know their own limitations in a professional capacity and that of their team. Regardless of how organised you are or are trying to be, there will invariably be some tasks that aren't important and end up wasting your time. You also need time to take some much-needed breaks.

There isn't anything you can do to overcome the limit. Unfortunately, there will never be sufficient time to do everything. Therefore, tasks must be prioritised according to their importance and urgency. Focus on planning your days such that a significant portion of your workday is dedicated to meaningful work and activities that generate value. This is the only means to get things done without burning yourself out, and it also sets a good example for your team to follow.

Develop Helpful Habits

When it comes to efficient productivity, you have two options available. The first one is to intentionally focus your effort and willpower on accomplishing a given task. The second is to do things automatically by developing helpful habits. You cannot become an organised manager if you don't adopt helpful core habits and routines. This also offers the structure needed to ensure your team's best performance, no matter the nature of the task at hand. Some basic core routines that can improve your productivity and that of the team include having daily stand-up meetings. Dedicate around 5 minutes to briefly discuss everything that happened the previous day and everything you wish to accomplish today.

This can be a little tricky with remote teams, especially with varying time zones. A good alternative is to invest in an online workplace, like Slack or Teams, for instance. This will allow for all updates, motivational speeches, or general get-togethers to be enjoyed by everyone, no matter what time of the day.

You should also have some planning sessions at the beginning of the week to determine the tasks your team has to complete within a given timeframe or the goals they need to achieve. This will help you regroup and take stock of certain aspects or variables that can be adjusted for better productivity. In addition, you can also encourage your team to visualise their workflow. Some other leadership routines you can develop include conducting one-on-one meetings with your team members or getting direct reports from them.

Work in the Flow

Getting into a flow is essential if you want to focus on important tasks at work. The flow is a brilliant experience that ensures you can add and deliver value quickly and efficiently. When you work in the flow, your overall productivity, creativity, and learning are improved and optimised. It's the ability to focus on the task at hand without letting peripheral thoughts undermine your productivity. When your focus becomes unidirectional, especially while working, your ability to achieve more increases, and you will concentrate better on a task and stay laser-focused on what you need to accomplish by the workday's end. After all, we only have limited resources at our disposal. Whether it is your time, energy, or financial resources, making the most of it is vital. Every day, try to set at least two two-hour blocks to accomplish as much as you can. At the same time, don't try to compensate and catch up if you miss out on a specific day or you risk burning yourself out.

Invest in Yourself

Another crucial aspect of becoming a highly organised manager is to invest in yourself. This isn't about investing in your skills or other work-related avenues. Instead, it's about taking care of your overall wellbeing. This includes your mental, physical, emotional, and spiritual health. When you care for yourself, you'll have more energy to get things done. Putting yourself first doesn't make you selfish. Instead, it is about sharpening the saw. For instance, tending to your physical and mental health reduces stress, bolsters your cognitive functioning, and enables you to stay positive and self-motivated. All these aspects improve your ability to regulate stress and emotions and make the most of every situation. When you learn to take care of yourself and make it a habit, you are leading by example. If you are functioning at your best, you can do your best in all instances.

Hiding behind excuses such as "I don't have time" or "I'm so overworked" doesn't justify you not taking the time to care for your physical and psychological health. After all, it's in your best interest to be and feel at ease, especially in the workplace. While exercising daily might not be workable with your schedule, it's important to engage in self-care rituals that will boost your general wellbeing and enable you to perform. This can be as easy as taking a walk around the block during your lunch break, eating more home-cooked meals, or practising short meditation sessions when you feel stress creeping up. There are countless ways to re-invite wellness into your routine for a genuinely productive and rewarding lifestyle.

Some Practical Tips

- Keep your desk clean and avoid working in a mess. When everything is in order in your workspace, you can stay focused. For instance, if the desk is cluttered with a mountain of files and only one of them is important, your chance of being distracted is much greater. Similarly, if you waste time looking around or searching for things, it will cripple your productivity. This can all be avoided by keeping your workspace organised and orderly.

- Make decluttering your space a habit. Whether it is documents, files, notes, or anything else, you can migrate these online. Everything can be stored in digital clouds, which reduces the need for physical storage. Online storage options make it easier to access information instantly and whenever the need arises. It is also easier to keep things organised and your mind clear in a decluttered space.

We all experience productivity at different times of the day. Whether it is in the early morning or the evening, plan your day in a way that aligns with your energy levels. For instance, if your energy levels are low during the afternoon, reserve less important work for this time. You should also identify what you can do to improve your energy levels. For example, you can reserve such low-energy periods for responding to emails or other low-priority tasks.

CHAPTER 2: GOAL SETTING

Everyone has different goals. That said, setting them is an art. It is a balancing act and an interesting process. We all have dreams we want to achieve. However, without setting goals, these dreams will just be that - dreams. The goals that you established for yourself must not only support the company mission on the work front, but they must be your own personal aspirations as well. Without fulfilling this condition, the act of setting them becomes an exercise of checking the boxes.

A simple yet effective technique is to use the SMART technique. This means setting goals that are Small, Measurable, Attainable, Relevant, and Time-bound. Unless a goal fulfils all these conditions, achieving it becomes more challenging. Regardless of how big or challenging, anything you want to achieve can be broken down into smaller targets. Similarly, unless you can measure the progress you are making, it becomes virtually impossible to determine how far you have come or the distance to be covered to achieve what you set for yourself. When the goal is measurable in quantifiable terms, necessary action can be taken to bring about changes. Also, it must be realistic or attainable. There is no point in chasing anything unrealistic. In fact, it's a recipe for failure. The goal must have some relevance or value to you. If this element is missing, the motivation needed to keep going diminishes, especially when obstacles crop up. This, in turn, reduces the chances of success. Finally, the goal must be time-bound. Without a deadline or a time limit to accomplish it, procrastination creeps in, and other distractions take priority. So, before you use any of the suggestions mentioned in this chapter, you must first ensure you set SMART goals.

Get Some Clarity

Before you can establish your desired targets, you must have some clarity about your function as a manager, along with your responsibilities, role, and purpose. Unless you are aware of all this, the goal will not be relevant. It only makes sense you know the purpose of your mission within any organisation before attempting to take things to the next level - something too many overlook despite having the best intentions. Also, you need to ensure that your goals do not impede your work or hamper your role as a manager. Instead, they need to be in perfect synchronisation with these considerations. So, you need clarity before you can get started. Without this, any goal you establish will become difficult to achieve. Once you have clarity about the specific and measurable things you can improve upon or learn, your chance of success will automatically increase.

Talk to Others

Two heads are better than one when it comes to problem-solving. When you are trying to establish goals or if you notice you are struggling to do so, talking to others always helps. It doesn't have to be your team members. Instead, you can speak to your superiors or peers. Solicit other managers who are in the same stage as you. Talking to them will give you different perspectives about the areas you can concentrate on. The input received from others can define your goals. You might not even realise there are certain opportunities you have overlooked or thought about because of your current line of thought. Ultimately, seeking help or support from people outside your immediate professional circle can open you up to a world of knowledge and expertise, which can strengthen your ability to plan clear and achievable goals in the long run.

Elements You Can Control

When it comes to establishing and following goals, you will need a plan of action. This plan must take into consideration not just the elements you can control, but the ones you cannot as well. While doing this is difficult, it is necessary to improve your chances of success. You don't have to worry too much about the factors or elements you cannot control. Instead, you need to plan and prepare for them. When you are prepared, even if it is only mental preparedness, your ability to deal with the obstacle, challenge, or problem you experience later on increases; this ensures that you are on the right track and are not getting distracted. It also prevents your motivation levels from dropping while pursuing the goal in question.

Career Path

While establishing goals, consider your career path in the long run. Ask yourself what your ideal professional role is and the qualifications or skills needed to achieve it. You need to line up the personal goals you are establishing to give yourself a chance to gain the necessary skills. This also improves the motivation required to stick to your plan of action.

Because it isn't uncommon for people to want a substantial life to change well into their professional career, it is imperative that you re-evaluate your professional circumstances every few months or years. Ask yourself whether your current occupation is fulfilling and rewarding and whether it allows you to develop strong financial independence and stability. If it is the case, then more power to you, and you know you are on the right track.

On the contrary, if you feel your job is no longer granting you that initial satisfaction of knowing that what you do is useful or rewarding, it might be time to reconsider your priorities and seek better opportunities elsewhere. In the end, honesty and openness about your achievements will invariably drive your progress and development.

Big Picture Matters

Productivity and proficiency are essential attributes of a successful manager. That said, in terms of growth in your professional career, it is not just restricted to productivity and proficiency. You need an idea of the experiences and skills required to advance your chosen career. Regardless of your goal, make sure to participate in professional seminars and educational opportunities whenever possible. Continued learning is needed for your ability to climb the corporate ladder. However, it isn't about becoming complacent in your role as a manager. Doing it to the best of your abilities is important. Keeping the big picture in mind when pursuing your career advancement will enable you to develop the skills and motivation needed to become to best manager you can be.

Understand Achievement

While establishing a goal, you should also consider what success and achievement look like to you. Evidently, your definition of success won't be the same as that of your co-workers or team members. It means you will need to go beyond the SMART technique you were introduced to earlier. You need to think about and visualise what form your success will take. What are the things you can do to step into the flow state? What can you do to work more efficiently? Hold on to the visualisation of the goal to find the motivation needed to keep going. Once you have a better grasp on your definition of success and achievement, creating goals that will allow you to accomplish them becomes easier.

Check-Ins

After you have established the goal and started working on it, you will need regular check-ins to see your progress regularly. Therefore, the goal must be measurable. Once a week, take some time for self-introspection and see how far you have advanced toward achieving the goal. During that time, consider any changes that need to be made or any solutions to obstacles or challenges you face. More often than not, the goal can change, which means the plan must be tweaked accordingly. Similarly, regular check-ins also give you better insight into what you can do differently to avoid facing similar obstacles in the future. Monitoring your progress also enables you to keep your energy levels in check, so you can better allocate your resources toward achieving that goal in the best and most efficient manner possible.

Support

Have you ever wondered how celebrities manage to look flawless at all times? They have a team of professionals supporting and catering to their needs and requirements. This is how they put their best foot forward. Likewise, if you want to be successful, you will need a support system or a team in place. Being surrounded by people who can support you in your professional endeavours is the best way to perform at your best. The same is needed whenever you are trying to achieve a goal. Even if you are the one focusing on improving your productivity at the workplace, other aspects of your life must be taken care of. This is why you need a support system.

Whether it comprises your teammates, colleagues, or even family members, friends, and loved ones, they will all come in handy. To illustrate this point, if you want to improve your golfing skill, you'll need an instructor to teach you the basics and help hone your skills. Similarly, you need allies to achieve your personal and professional goals. Whether it is a network of professionals inside or outside the organisation, always make sure you build yourself a strong support team. They will grant you strength and motivation when you are running low, which will help re-centre your energy and focus on what matters most. You can also go to them for advice. Knowing that you are not alone and that others are supporting you by themselves can boost your confidence in a way you never imagined.

Comparison

When you establish goals at work, it gives you the tools needed to map out the big-picture targets you want to achieve. However, there will be other things you need to focus on as well. This can become a source of distraction that can unnecessarily increase your stress levels, which can become overwhelming when left unregulated. As such, you will need to periodically compare what you are doing and what you should be doing. In other words, "what is" and "what should be" side by side will help you evaluate your performance and see how far you have come to achieve your objectives. Once you are aware of this, you can take the necessary action to focus on important tasks that add value and meaning to your life. Check your daily to-do list and ensure it aligns with your established goals. A sure-fire way to accomplish your vision is to include more activities that will bring you closer to your goals while minimising distractions.

Count the Wins

It is no secret that managers are busy most of the time. Sometimes, it might feel as though you are busy but have nothing to show for it. In such instances, thinking about what you have accomplished can become difficult. This becomes even more challenging, especially if you are dealing with obstacles preventing you from achieving your goals. That said, even if you are struggling at the moment, there are likely things that you are doing correctly. This includes things that are going right for you and wins that have come your way. It serves you well to remember all that you have sacrificed and gone through to be where you are right now. You must keep track of your accomplishments to motivate yourself to follow your dreams and goals. Don't focus on things that are not working for you, but count your blessings and be happy about the ones that are going right.

CHAPTER 3: TIME MANAGEMENT

Learning to manage your time is one of the most important skills anyone can have, especially in the workplace. After all, the time you have helps determine the life you are leading. We all have an equal number of hours to accomplish various tasks that require our attention. However, whether you succeed in this endeavour depends on how you utilise the time available. Whether you are just starting your managerial role or require a refresher, it is never too late to learn and apply efficient time management skills. This is needed to move ahead quickly in your career.

Before you go over the different suggestions included in this chapter, here is a simple technique that can optimise the 24 hours you have to make the most of the time available. This technique is known as the Eisenhower matrix, and it was developed by former U.S. President Dwight Eisenhower.

He broke down time management into four important groups as follows.

1. Do first
2. Schedule
3. Delegate
4. Don't do

All the time management skills discussed here fall somewhere within this matrix. As mentioned, you will need to divide the tasks into different categories for better time management. Now, let's get started.

Plan the Goals

To manage your time efficiently, you must have goals in place. These will provide clear direction and precious guidance for whatever you want to accomplish. As such, you need to establish daily, weekly, monthly, and even yearly goals for yourself. This is how you know you are on the right track and are making the most of your time. Without goals, every action you take might or might not produce the results you desire. To reduce this incertitude, you need some basic goals, but this isn't just about establishing a goal. As explained, you need to ensure they are small, measurable, achievable, relevant, and time-bound. Vague or unachievable objectives won't take you far on the road to success. As long as it fulfils all these SMART conditions, your ability to achieve it improves.

Good Communication

If you are struggling to manage your time properly, one thing that invariably suffers is your ability to communicate effectively and efficiently with those around you. Communication isn't effective unless the person you are addressing has not fully understood what you are saying. For this reason, it's important that you adopt a clear communication style, to the point, and be action-oriented. Remember that people always respond well to those who can express themselves and easily get a message across. Failing to meet this essential criterion will put the brakes on your growth as a manager.

By improving your communication skills, you will be better able to manage your time. Excellent communication is useful when establishing and implementing your priorities. This means that you are not squandering precious hours on immaterial tasks and activities or ones that don't add value. Instead, you can focus on things that need to be done, boosting your productivity in incredible ways.

Staying Organised

Your ability to stay organised is a no-brainer if you want to manage your time in the most efficient way possible. As we all know, chaos is a time management killer. It might not look like it on the surface, but it ends up sapping your productivity. Whether it is your desk, a list of tasks to be completed, or anything else at work, everything around you must be organised. This also ensures that the things you need are readily available at your disposal and that you aren't wasting time searching for them when the need arises. Down the line, adopting this habit of keeping everything organised will set a superb example for others to follow and earn you the respect and admiration of your collaborators.

Start Delegating

As we have previously seen, you cannot become an efficient time manager unless you delegate tasks and understand the importance of doing so. Being a manager doesn't mean you have to do everything on your own. Instead, identify tasks and activities you believe others are qualified to carry out and start delegating. This applies not just to your professional life, but to your personal life as well. The delegation also means that the tasks that require your attention are important and will be completed without delay. In many ways, it improves your chance of success when it comes to achieving your goals. Besides, you will be in a position where you can empower those who work under your direct supervision by entrusting them with specific tasks.

Proper Schedule

If you were in charge of constructing a building, you wouldn't think about installing the roof without the foundation and walls in place first, would you? This is the same logic that you must use when scheduling your time. It means that tasks must get the time needed and should be carried out in a specific order. The first part of the Eisenhower matrix you were introduced to earlier includes tasks that fall into the "Do first" category. It means that, regardless of how long your to-do list is, you need to start with the activities that are of utmost importance and priority. Think of this as a way to establish a solid foundation for everything that follows. After this, you can knock out the other tasks on the list. Unless you learn to prioritise the time available and schedule it properly, you cannot become an excellent time manager.

Multitasking

A common idea most people like to adhere to is that multitasking means enhanced productivity. If you take a moment and think about it, it simply results in a waste of time. Think of your attention and focus as a bucket full of water. Every task you do puts a hole in it. If there are multiple holes in the bucket, there will not be any water left inside. Therefore, if you are trying to do more than one thing at once, you aren't getting more done. Instead, it will cause a situation where you have got nothing done altogether. For instance, if you are working on an urgent presentation and then focus on replying to your emails because your phone just chimed, then you have completed neither of these tasks in the allotted time. To avoid these situations, stick to the list of tasks you have created, and get the most important ones out of the way before moving on to the next one. Your overall productivity will improve by getting things done in an orderly fashion. It also ensures that you have optimised the time available to you. On top of that, you will train your mind to only focus on one thing at a time, which will significantly boost your concentration and allow you to complete your checklist without delay.

When to Let Go

Whether you are a freshly appointed manager or have been at it for a while, there will be different things you need to accomplish on a daily basis. However, if you notice that the list of tasks that fall into the "must-be-done" category is becoming increasingly long, then it is an indicator of two things. The first possibility is that you are not managing your time as efficiently as you should be. The second possibility is that you have prioritised the wrong tasks to begin with. This isn't something to beat yourself up about, especially as a new manager, since mastering time management is often a game of trial and error. You must find a rhythm and organisation style that works for you and enables you to get things done.

If you aren't managing your time properly, start from the beginning and review the entire process. Understand that you are not superhuman and that you have your limits. Otherwise, you will end up overworking yourself, which can cause burnout. Aside from that, don't forget that you only have fixed hours at your disposal. You don't have to try to do every task by yourself. Instead, delegate strategically so that you are focusing only on important ones.

80/20 Rule

Also known as the Pareto principle, this rule suggests that 80% of the results obtained are usually from around 20% of the actions or efforts you make. The other 20% of the results you get will account for the rest, 80% of your actions or behaviours. Now, are you wondering how this is associated with time management? This essentially means that all the tasks must be prioritised and fall into the must-be-done category, which might account for only 20% of your job responsibility but produce significant results. It also means that the rest of your duties that account for 80% of your job profile can be delegated. In that optic, start prioritising your days such that the big tasks are out of the way and a significant chunk of your daily tasks are completed.

Take Breaks

Time management is not about engaging yourself every waking minute of the day. It's also not restricted to just making the most of the time available. In reality, an important aspect of it is taking regular breaks. You don't have to work like a non-stop freight train to convince yourself that you are up to any challenge that comes your way. You are allowed to take a couple of moments for yourself and enjoy much-needed breaks when you feel the urge to do so. There will be instances when your plate is too full, which is precisely when you must take a break. Kick back a little and re-energise your mind before getting back to the task at hand. This improves your efficiency and ensures you do not burn yourself out, which can have serious consequences. Don't feel guilty when you need to take a break. Instead, understand that you have earned it. If not, it will eventually take a toll on your overall sense of wellbeing and your physical health.

With all that in mind, make it a point not to over-schedule your workday and to always leave some time for yourself. For instance, you can dedicate a few precious minutes to clear your mind, perform deep breathing exercises, take a walk, have a power smoothie, or send a voice message to your loved ones to let them know how your day is going. Whether in your personal, professional, or educational life, breaks are needed. When you schedule some downtime for yourself, it encourages you to feel and work better.

You will learn more about managing your time effectively and efficiently in the next part of this book. For now, let's get back to self-management skills.

CHAPTER 4: SELF-MOTIVATION

Self-motivated managers are positive and friendly leaders with exemplary communication skills. They believe in themselves and project confidence. In that sense, self-motivated leaders are enthusiastic about their work and inspire their teams to do better at every opportunity they get. Such individuals are humble and energetic and aren't afraid of making mistakes or accepting responsibility, and they don't blame others and constantly work on improving themselves. Great managers are also resilient enough to bounce back from obstacles and failures without giving up. A lot of adjectives can describe a self-motivated manager. If you want to become one, you need to learn to stay motivated. While it can certainly challenge to approach every professional or personal situation with a positive, self-encouraging mindset, your ability to find motivation and strength throughout your endeavours will make you a manager that people look up to.

Becoming an exemplary manager is a very demanding process that requires a great deal of perseverance and hard work. Regardless of the challenges and obstacles you face, you will need to stay positive and motivated. This is needed because others are counting on you and rely on you for guidance. An important part of a manager's job profile is to motivate their team. Before they can start doing this, they need to learn to motivate themselves. This is especially crucial when plans don't work out or things become challenging. This chapter provides practical suggestions to build self-motivation and become the best and most inspiring manager you can be.

Objectives and Key Results

One of the best ways to stay motivated is by establishing objectives and key results. Objectives and key results are abbreviated as OKRs. Focus on setting between 3 and 5 OKRs for yourself. This not only helps you stay motivated and enables your team to achieve their objectives, but also improves their overall productivity. The great thing about establishing OKRs is that they encourage you to focus on things that need to be done and the steps to achieve them. When you have something to work toward, your ability to stay on track increases. When you can see your progress and effectively measure it, your motivation level will reach new heights. And as the objectives you wish to achieve are getting challenging, it becomes an exciting and valuable learning opportunity. This, by itself, will renew your motivation levels and enable you to push forward.

Reward Yourself

Whenever you successfully achieve something as a manager, don't forget to reward yourself. If you are harsh on yourself when you make a mistake, it is important that you praise yourself when you do something right. This isn't about being vain or trying to stay modest. Instead, it's about self-awareness and recognising what you are doing well. As leaders, we forget there is more to the role than simply celebrating the achievement of our teams. If your team does something right, you have a role to play in that success. That said, it doesn't mean you should go overboard and reward yourself for simply getting out of bed. Instead, whenever you reach a specific milestone, celebrate it duly. Rejoice in the little victories that come your way, and the motivation you need will increase. Perhaps you can treat yourself to a day at the spa, eat at your favourite restaurant, or do anything else along those lines. Whenever you do or achieve something meaningful at work, celebrate it in a way that makes you feel good. In the same way, you would reward yourself with a well-deserved break from the job. Make sure to honour your efforts with an activity that brings you joy and allows you to contemplate everything you have achieved for yourself, your team, and the company. That way, you will always have something to look forward to once you have hit a milestone or achieved an important goal.

Find Some Inspiration

You are probably used to playing the role of the person who others look up to. They look up to you when they need inspiration, encouragement, or motivation. With that in mind, you will also need someone who can do this for you. Therefore, look for someone who inspires you. Whether it is motivational speakers, successful entrepreneurs, or even leaders from history, find a meaningful figure whose work or achievements resonate with you and your vision of success. Alternatively, you can watch motivational videos online or read books and autobiographies from famous public figures. Having a positive role model will also help improve your behaviour and actions for the better. You can use their stories to overcome any challenges and discover your true potential. In the end, it will also help you remember where you came from and everything you have achieved so far in your career.

Work-Life Balance

One of the common reasons most people lose motivation or feel stuck in their jobs is a lack of work-life balance. Without this much-needed balance, you cannot have mental peace. It isn't just about getting ahead in your career. You need to have a personal life too. Balancing your personal and professional life is essential to your overall health and wellbeing. Your ability to separate your professional duties from your personal obligations will ensure you maintain a sense of structure, promoting the organisation, productivity, and more.

As a manager, you might focus on improving your team's performance or helping them. But you need to help yourself too. Don't forget about yourself in this process. The results you are trying to achieve should not be for the sake of your quality of life. Instead, opt for their co-existence.

Do not overwork yourself and burn yourself out to prove to yourself that you can "do it all." Set time for your personal life, relationships, goals, projects, etc. You will learn more about maintaining this balance in the latter part of this book.

Delegation

Regardless of how big or small the team is, it brings with it a different set of responsibilities. Because of the pressure, there will be times when you do not feel like completing certain tasks. If you believe someone in your team can take care of it, delegate. No rule says you need to do everything on your own. Learning to delegate is an important aspect of your role as a manager. If you refuse to assign responsibility to others, you'll be stuck with an ever-increasing pile of tasks to be completed. This, in turn, increases the risk of complete burnout. Whether it is a routine task or an important responsibility, make it a point to delegate as much as possible. This ensures that the most important issues get your undivided attention. Also, when you delegate, it improves team morale, teaches them responsibility, and gives them a chance to learn and grow. This allows everyone to benefit and shows how dependable they can be in the workplace.

Have Fun

It's no secret that certain occupations can suck the joy out of being in the workplace. A lifeless work environment can take a great toll on everybody's morale and motivation, hindering your team's ability to achieve goals and get things done productively. So, along with taking advantage of the different suggestions mentioned until now, focus on having fun at work. Have you ever heard the saying, "All work and no play make Jack a dull boy?" To ensure this doesn't happen to you, engage in communal activities with your team members. It fosters a more robust support network between the team members, encourages team spirit, and ensures everyone is involved. This is also an excellent way to bring the entire team together and improve their sense of motivation along with yours.

Mentor Others

No matter how much you love your job, there will come a time when things become a little repetitive. This will happen regardless of how invested you are in the job. There will be days when trying to find the passion you felt when you started working can feel like an impossible task, and you might not even remember what it feels like. In such instances, the best thing you can do to break out of the rut is to find someone else to mentor.

Find someone who is getting started and take them under your wing. The best thing about new individuals or interns is that they're not only motivated to learn, but they are also willing to work twice as hard as anyone else to prove their worth. Whether they are fresh graduates or trying to change their careers, find someone you can teach and help adjust to their new role. Chances are, they will be extremely grateful that you volunteer your time to help them out, which will showcase how caring and devoted you are as a manager. You can then use their excitement and determination to reignite the spark of your own motivation. Guiding, mentoring, and passing on your experience and knowledge to someone else helps renew your sense of motivation. Seeing them advance in their careers and do well is also inspiring.

CHAPTER 5: STRESS MANAGEMENT

Stress is not only common, but an undeniable part of life. It hampers your productivity and impedes effective time management and productivity. We all deal with multiple stressors daily, whether on the job, at home, or online. Depending on what we do for a living and the responsibilities entrusted to us, we all experience varying degrees of stress on a daily basis. However, the stress level managers are exposed to is generally on the higher end of the scale. Whether you are managing your financial portfolio, employees, or even daily chores, there is much to do. All the tasks, activities, and processes demand time, attention, effort, and accountability. While doing all this, you still need to consider the adaptability needed to adjust to the ever-changing conditions and external factors beyond your control. This, in turn, can add to the stress you are already under.

Excess stress is highly detrimental to your overall sense of wellbeing. Whether it is your mental, physical, or emotional health, stress affects it all. Its effects are severe and far-reaching, from increased risk of cardiovascular disorders and blood pressure to headaches, insomnia, and an inability to focus. Now, since we cannot eliminate stress, learning to regulate it is vital to both your personal and professional success. In this chapter, you will learn about simple and practical techniques for stress management. Hopefully, by the end of this read, you will have gained a deeper understanding of how to identify the sources of stress in your life and how to address them effectively and durably.

Identify the Trigger

You cannot deal with the stress you're experiencing unless you can identify what triggers it. A stressor, or stress trigger, is much like the trigger for a gun. Unless you pull the trigger, the bullet is not fired. Similarly, different things can trigger your stress. To identify your triggers, self-introspection is needed. It is important to look into what you think may cause you stress, whether it's high workloads, tight deadlines, meetings with shareholders, upcoming large-scale events, etc. Some of it can be attributed to your personal circumstances, such as relationships, family pressures, and more. So, make it a habit to take a step back and objectively evaluate what may add unnecessary stress to your life. You can also start journaling to help notice any patterns you may have overlooked. Certain situations or even people can make you feel anxious, worried, impatient, restless, or irritable, affecting your ability to stay organised and productive. If so, then make a note of it. This will help determine what is causing your stress. Perhaps a conversation with your boss makes you stressed. Or maybe the thought of managing your finances is the cause. Whatever the reason, the first step is to learn to identify your trigger. Without this, you cannot fully handle, much less overcome, the stress you feel on the spot.

Counteract Stress

Since we cannot eliminate stress, you must focus on managing it. Now that you better understand your stressors or triggers, it's time to learn to handle them. What is your usual response to stress? We all react to it in different, often surprising ways. Some people get irritated, while others might resort to emotional binge-eating or engaging in other unhealthy behaviours or distractions. Invariably, acknowledging the stress is the first step in counteracting it. Once you have identified that and your natural or typical responses to it, you can work on finding healthier and more sustainable ways to ease the stress you experience in a professional context.

When it comes to stress management, there is no right or wrong way. However, some mechanisms are more helpful than others. For instance, if you think reaching for a cigarette will help reduce your stress, you need to think again. Developing an unhealthy habit to cope with the stress you are experiencing further worsens the stress you are already under. Also, unhelpful habits have long-lasting repercussions for your wellbeing. Some useful techniques that can be used to deal with stress include mindfulness meditation, deep breathing, listening to relaxing music, or even going for a short walk. The simplest method of all is mindfulness meditation.

To do this, remove yourself from the stressful situation you are in. Find a quiet spot for yourself, close your eyes, and focus on your breathing. Breathe in deeply, and as you breathe out, visualise that you are expelling all the stress from your body. Do this until your mind goes blank and you feel calm. Once you are calmer, you can get back to the situation at hand. Of course, it will take a great deal of practice before you can reap the full benefits of meditation, so don't expect to get it all right from the get-go. Give yourself enough time for your body and mind to adjust to this state where it can let go and start fresh. With practice and advice from research and professionals, you will successfully incorporate meditation into your daily routine and feel its benefit in your wellbeing and work performance.

Avoid Perfectionism

Most of us strive for perfection. In one form or another, we want to be perfect. Unfortunately, perfection is nothing but a mirage. It doesn't exist. All you can do is your best. Chasing perfection not only sets you up for failure, but it can also become a source of incredible stress. This self-inflicted pressure can leave you unable to even carry out simple tasks without worrying that a few details might ruin the flow and quality of your work. As a manager, you might feel that it is your responsibility to ensure that everything goes as planned at all times. Remember that life is not always smooth sailing. There will be storms you need to withstand.

When you are chasing excellence, striving for perfection is common. However, perfectionism is an illusion that creates an all-or-nothing mentality. This mentality makes you believe that anything that is less than 100% right or complete as per your standards equals failure and is unacceptable. In reality, mistakes are bound to happen, and failure is a part of the journey toward success. Therefore, let go of this attitude and, instead, put your best foot forward. It is a way to learn and grow, so cut yourself some slack and stop chasing perfection. Ultimately, coming to terms with the fact that you won't always be able to deliver flawlessly, impeccable work will help you accept nothing is ever perfect, even for the most brilliant managers out there.

Talk It Out

A common mistake people make is burying their stress. Not talking about it or expressing it worsens the situation. If you are ignoring a problem or at least trying to, remember that it will not be miraculously solved. Instead, you need to face it head-on. The longer you ignore it, the more stress you will experience. A simple yet effective means to break the cycle is by talking about it to others. Whether it is a friend, relative, or anyone else, share your worries with them. It will not only make you feel better, but you might get some refreshing perspectives.

Viewing a situation from a single point of view can blind you to other important considerations. Start accepting that you might have missed certain things, which you will only realise while talking about them. Also, when you are open about the stress you are experiencing, you might accidentally yet, fortunately, stumble upon what is causing it. Another benefit of sharing is that it helps you to see things more clearly. What seems like a disaster in your head might not actually warrant putting yourself in complete disarray. Even if it doesn't solve the problem, simply talking about it will take a great load off your shoulders.

Naturally, not that you should air out any feeling or sentiment without considering the repercussions of what you say or to whom. As a manager, you must be tactful with others, but you also owe that tactfulness to yourself as well. For that reason, try to formulate what you are feeling as best as you can and consider whom you are sharing this information with before doing so.

Healthy Lifestyle Changes

Anyone can benefit from making changes toward a healthy lifestyle. Leading a healthier life is a superb way to address and manage any stress you experience. It includes basic things like getting good quality sleep, eating healthy and well-balanced meals, exercising regularly, and staying hydrated. This might sound trivial, but they are the most commonly overlooked aspects of healthy living. When you focus on taking care of your health and developing meaningful habits, your overall sense of wellbeing improves. Physical and mental health go hand-in-hand. In other words, your ability to cope with stress becomes second nature. It will also improve your mood and make you more resistant to stress.

Adopting these habits is not an overnight process. That said, all the efforts you make right now to do this will be repaid a hundredfold in the future. Regardless of how healthy or active you think you are at the moment, committing to a healthier lifestyle with little steps and tweaks to your routine will eventually translate into a more rewarding and gratifying lifestyle. Don't hesitate to ask people in your entourage what they do to stay healthy and how they cope with the stress of daily life, and draw inspiration from others' experiences to forge your own lifestyle routine.

Be Less of a Manager

Paradoxically, if you want to reduce the stress you are experiencing, you need to be less of a manager. Does that sound counterintuitive? Your stress can be a combination of all your managerial duties. If you take a moment to think about this, it makes sense. Not all your duties are equally important. However, they still need to be done. Looking at an overcrowded to-do list can quickly become overwhelming for you. Whether you have a hands-on or hands-off approach to your managerial role, you will still want to ensure the work goes on smoothly. There is no one-formula-fits-all approach to the problems you face. Instead of stressing yourself out, thinking about every single thing that needs to be managed, play the role of a collaborator. This, in turn, will help improve your efficiency, promote better time management, and reduce your stress.

Seek Help

There is certainly no harm in asking for help when you need it. It doesn't matter which stage of your career you are in - we all need a little boost at one point or another. If it feels like the stress you are experiencing is too much or you cannot handle it, then seek help. The current work culture that most of us are exposed to is challenging, demanding, and overwhelming. In some ways, it exposes us to even more stressors. Remember that you don't have to do everything on your own. Instead, you can start strategizing and delegating responsibilities to lighten your workload.

CHAPTER 6: DECISION MAKING

From the moment you wake up, until you go to sleep, you make all sorts of decisions. You might not even consciously think about most of them. What to eat, what to wear, what route to take to work, or even what time to sleep are some examples of decisions we make every day. Some are small, while others are major, and some can be made with barely a thought, while others must be intentional. For managers, decision-making is one aspect that requires great attention to detail. It's the ability to make choices that will yield the best results for your organisation without compromising work quality or effective time management. As it happens, decision-making is not an innate skill. Rather, it is one that we learn from experiences and previous situations. The good news is that any manager or aspiring management can do a lot to improve their ability to make wise and judicious choices for increased productivity and performance.

There might be instances when having to decide can feel downright dreadful. When you are in the decision-making process, there can be a lot at stake. It automatically puts you in a position of responsibility where you need to be a good leader. There will also be instances when you do not have the sufficient time required to carefully think things through or analyse the facts before deciding. In parallel, there will be times when the information directly available to you doesn't make decision-making a straightforward process. Worrying whether or not you are making the right decision can increase self-doubt and mess up your flow of work or ability to get things done. That said, as the decision-maker, you have opportunities that can result in success or failure. Making a poor decision is always a possibility, and therefore, it's important to train yourself to become an efficient decision-maker. The process of how or when to decide can be a little overwhelming, but by following the basic framework discussed in this chapter, you can become a better decision-maker.

Identify

When it comes to decision-making, the first step is to decide where the decision needs to be made. This gives you a better idea of the problem you are actively trying to solve. If you are not aware of what you are dealing with or the situation itself, then make sure you take the time required to investigate. Unless you are familiar with the given area or situation, you cannot make a good decision. So, make it a habit to identify the context in which you are called upon to decide, whether that pertains to managing client deliverables, prioritising your time, or any other activity around the workplace.

Review

Once you are aware of where to focus and what decision must be made, it's time to brainstorm. You cannot make an informed decision without considering all the relevant and available information. There will be plenty of information and data to go through, which can become quite chaotic to navigate and weigh out. The best way to stay on top of it and ensure that you are organised is by using basic strategies such as mind mapping, drawing a flowchart, or even using coloured post-its. Depending on what kind of learner you are (visual, reader, writer, hands-on, etc.), it's important that you find a system that enables you to maximise your efficiency in the face of the decision-making process. It will ensure that you do not lose sight of essential information or documents.

Alternatives

While deciding, consider some of the potential solutions and outcomes of a specific decision. After reviewing the information carefully, you will generally have more than one option. Now is not the time to worry about which is the best choice. Instead, it's about asking questions and listening to the feedback you receive. Talk about and discuss these alternatives with your team members or any other trusted individuals within the organisation, as there will probably be a lot to think over. Also, the different alternatives you consider must be in sync with your organisational methods and goals.

Evidence

Once you are aware of all the solutions and outcomes in front of you, weigh their pros and cons. Chances are, even your competitors will have dealt with such decisions at some point. Consider their outcomes and the decisions they made, whether that pertains to a marketing strategy, an expansion plan, or online visibility, for example. After this, carefully go through the probable wins and losses associated with each of the possible alternatives. Be sure to factor in how the specific decision will affect your team members and any other stakeholders. If the decision is associated with the change, consider what you need to do to adapt to it and how they will do it. Don't be in a hurry at this stage. The decision you make must make you confident. While it is entirely normal to have doubts, any reservations you have about your decision should not throw you into a state of mental paralysis, leaving you unable to concentrate or realistically anticipate the outcomes of that decision. You need to be comfortable with what you have decided based on the steps mentioned until now.

Choice

You have made it to the stage where a final decision must be made. After weighing the evidence and reviewing the information along with the alternatives, it's time to decide and take a firm stand. When doing this, learn to trust yourself. Be confident in your abilities and listen to your gut. Remember that you are qualified to make this call. It's no secret that making a choice can be frustratingly pressuring. Depending on a variety of aspects, such as your work style, ethics, personality, and the responsibilities entrusted to you, you might be second-guessing yourself. That is normal. However, as a sound and organised manager, you must believe in your ability to formulate a well-reasoned decision that will benefit the organisation as a whole. So, trust your judgment and don't seek to make a "perfect" decision because, as we've seen, there is no such thing.

Act

A decision without action is nonsensical. Now, it is time to implement the decision. To that end, focus on creating a plan that will bring your team and organisation closer to its goals. Strategic planning can take time, but it's a key ingredient for a successful outcome. Also, execution matters because even the best plan can fail when executed poorly. While the specifics are entirely up to you, it's important that you include any interested parties in your plan of action so that everyone is in the loop and knows what to expect as a result of your managerial decision.

Reflect

The last step of the decision-making process is reflection. It is not just about deciding and moving on to the next ones. Rather than take the expediting approach, take some time to review and reflect. You might even identify a better course of action for any future decision or fix issues that hindered the final results and outcomes. Think about all the skills that came in useful and what you would want to do differently the next time around. The goal of this step is not to determine whether you made the right choice. Instead, it is about honestly considering whether you have done the best and about things that worked and things that didn't.

For instance, you can consider questions such as: *Was the problem identified solved? How good was the process of information gathering? Were the goals you established fulfilled?* If you made mistakes at any stage, make a note of them. By learning from every decision you make as a manager; you stand a significant chance of improving your decision-making skills.

Challenges to Overcome

When it comes to efficient decision-making, the common challenges most managers face are as follows.

- Having too much information or too little knowledge can be downright puzzling. Only with practice can you efficiently prioritise and select crucial pieces of information. This, in turn, makes decision-making easier. If needed, conduct more research before deciding.
- It is important to be confident about the decisions you make. That said, overconfidence can be detrimental. Even when you are doing your best, there will be instances when the decision isn't the right one. This is part and parcel of life. So, don't forget to acknowledge the possibility of making errors.
- An important aspect of the decision-making process is to correctly identify a problem or situation where a decision has to be made. If you

- misidentify, you cannot expect the final decision to yield the desired results.
- The final challenge you need to overcome is to ensure everyone is on board with the decision you made. You are the final decision-maker for your team. However, unless the entire team is kept in the loop, collaboration is not possible. In this process, you'll need to be transparent and ensure that your team is aware of how the decision was made, as well as the criteria for making it.

Making choices daily is an essential aspect of your role as a manager. Once you learn to identify, review, and act on the decision you have made, it will become easier for you to formulate coherent choices that everyone can accept and get behind when needed. Remember that a critical aspect of this is honesty and transparency and that you cannot promote a healthy collaborative framework without including others and explaining your process. You owe your collaborators a certain level of disclosure, which, when you deliver, makes them trust you and be more inclined to accept your decision.

CHAPTER 7: ACCOUNTABILITY

Who wouldn't feel happy when their plans work and they achieve the goals they have set for themselves? By contrast, no one is happy with themselves when they don't achieve the above. In fact, most people will look for someone or something to blame when things don't work out as they intend. If you are eager to take responsibility or credit for all the things that go right, do not shy away from taking responsibility when things don't work out as planned, either.

This is where accountability steps in. Holding yourself accountable means you can efficiently manage not just work but other aspects of your life and fulfil all your obligations. It is based on consistent self-reflection of your actions, thoughts, and general conduct. It is about accepting the outcomes of your decisions and the process that led you to formulate them. When you learn to hold yourself accountable, your ability to complete tasks effectively improves. It also gives you an improved sense of control over yourself and your life. It enables you to evaluate your quality of work, support others in their efforts, and boost your self-confidence. Moreover, taking responsibility also allows you to learn and develop self-management skills. If you want to improve your sense of accountability, start following the practical suggestions given in this chapter.

Being Resentful

Becoming resentful or resistant is common when responsibility is forced upon us. However, those who are accountable are not only willing to actively take on responsibilities but manage themselves to ensure they fulfil these responsibilities. Remember that once your name is associated with a specific initiative or a responsibility, it is your duty to fulfil it. It is no one else's job to do but your own. No one has to worry about its completion other than you.

When things go wrong, looking at who or what to blame is merely a waste of time. Understand that if you have to do something and it does not go according to your plan, or a problem is created, then no one else is to be blamed. Don't blame others for your inaction, wrong decisions, and missteps. You cannot improve your sense of accountability if you are constantly looking for other things to blame. Don't excuse yourself based on any external influences. Instead, analyse why the problem cropped up and then work on fixing it.

As an effective manager, you need to fulfil your responsibilities and achieve your objectives. However, when they are no longer useful, they no longer serve any purpose. Everything you do must be done within a specific time limit. Pushing it to later is of no use, either. If you want to be accountable, you must ensure that you are always punctual. Live your life such that you are not just conscious about wasting your own time, but that of others around you as well. This will make you more trustworthy, too.

Accountability Is Key

Many things are beyond your control. External factors can change in the blink of an eye. That said, there are certain things that you can control. Instead of getting overwhelmed, focus on those. You are the writer of your destiny. With a positive mindset and a pragmatic attitude, you can overcome most of the challenges that come your way. A highly accountable person doesn't have a victim mentality, which occurs when you believe you are at the mercy of factors beyond your control. Instead, focus on all that you can do to rise to the challenge and the circumstances. You don't have to wait to be monitored by others. Instead, focus on diligently doing the job assigned to you. This will improve your sense of accountability.

It's not just fate that is in your control, but your thoughts and emotions as well. When the stakes are high, emotions usually run high. If you are not careful, these emotions will start controlling your thoughts, actions, and behaviours. Since your ability to achieve your goals is related to your actions and behaviours, you need to be in control of them. Learning to regulate your feelings ensures your productivity is not derailed. Even when you are having a bad day, understand that your feelings are your own. Don't blame them on others. No one can make you feel something unless you allow yourself to feel it. Instead of assigning blame, take charge of your emotions. This will improve your sense of self-control and do wonders for your work productivity.

Working on your accountability becomes that much easier when you learn to manage your expectations. It is perfectly okay to aim high. That said, don't aim so high that it is not realistic or the goal itself is no longer workable, as this will set you up for failure. In such instances, taking accountability for your actions or inactions becomes extremely tricky. Do not do this to yourself. Instead, manage your expectations. Expectations are not just about yourself, but what you are expecting from others as well. You cannot control others.

We all love to be praised. We all want to be showered with accolades. Be that as it may, highly accountable people know that their sense of satisfaction stems from the inside. It doesn't matter what others feel or think about you or what you do. Instead, focus on how you feel after doing or not doing something. This is where a sense of accomplishment comes from. If you receive any praise for a job well done, it is nothing but a bonus, which you can use to boost your self-motivation and stay focused on bigger goals.

Along with punctuality, it is important that you establish a timeline for yourself. Your ability to manage time influences whether you can achieve your different goals. Your sense of accountability improves when you know you are the only one responsible for achieving your goals and dreams. This is your responsibility and no one else's.

CHAPTER 8: CONFIDENCE

Playing the role of a manager is not a simple task. It's not just your superiors who have huge expectations, but even those who are working under your leadership. At times, you might feel as though you are stuck between a rock and a hard place. In such instances, feeling confident is nearly impossible. However, this is one of those traits that attracts others to you. In management, this is vital. To provide a brief definition, confidence is simply your ability to have faith in your own skills, accomplishments, and goals. Some managers ooze it effortlessly, and their employees love and respect them. There are also know-it-all's who tend to be bossy and unappreciated by their teams. While the former is desirable, the latter isn't. By following the different suggestions given here, you can become more confident as a manager and be more efficient at your job.

Realistic Expectations

To build your confidence, you mustn't be unreasonably harsh on yourself. This means you shouldn't set unrealistic expectations. Most of us have unrealistic expectations when it comes to excelling at work. It's okay if you want to do your best at all times. Simultaneously, you mustn't set yourself up for failure. It's okay to set challenges, but losing sight of what's practical and realistic won't serve your work performance or professional development. Learn to trust your expectations to guarantee that you do not set yourself up for failure. Whether you need to change your timetable or allow yourself to make mistakes, go ahead and do it. It's okay to make mistakes, and it certainly is not the end of the road. Remember that every mistake is an opportunity for growth and development. Assuming you will be right all the time is a recipe for failure and burnout, so it is important to learn to manage your own expectations in order not to fall short. Also, trying to achieve unrealistic goals will reduce your self-confidence.

Your Merits

We all engage in self-doubt at some point. Don't doubt your capabilities as a manager or second-guess your potential. Understand that you got this job because of what you bring to the table and your merits. This position you are holding as a leader is not an accident or based on luck. Acknowledge the journey you underwent to get to where you are right now. You have what is needed to get the job done, and others believe in you. Now, it is time to prove them right. Whenever you feel that your sense of confidence is running low, reminding yourself of everything you have achieved until this point will make it that much easier for you to keep performing your duties.

Self-Awareness

In a similar vein, it is also important that you are self-aware. Self-awareness stems from not just being aware of your weaknesses, but also your strengths. Acknowledging and accepting your leadership strengths will improve your confidence. It also gives you the courage needed to face areas of development. In a way, it teaches you to improve yourself without putting yourself down. There are two steps when it comes to improving your self-awareness. The first is self-introspection, where you need to sit by yourself and carefully analyse your strengths and weaknesses. This can be a useful exercise to perform whenever you feel the need to re-centre your priorities or take stock of your current professional situation. The second step is to ask others for feedback and consider it. If there are a few co-workers you trust, solicit them about your general performance as a manager. Of course, it is essential that you keep an open mind, be ready to listen, and not hold anything against them in the future. As we mentioned, listening to someone else's perspectives can open you up to work habits or personality traits that you need to work on or develop. Once you do all this, you will be more aware of the areas where you excel and where there is room for improvement.

Project Confidence

"Fake it until you make it." Does that sound familiar? Well, it is time to do the same. There will be instances when you do not feel confident at all. Even then, projecting confidence does a lot. You are not the only person or manager who is unsure of themselves. This is extremely common. Have you ever seen people who seem effortlessly confident? It almost looks as if they were born with it. In reality, they can do this because they have learned to fake it until they make it. Even when you are terrified on the inside, you can still project confidence. To feel confident, focus on your physical appearance. It may sound rather vain, but it is incredibly helpful.

Do certain clothes or accessories make you feel more comfortable and confident? If you have heard that appearances do not matter, let go of this notion. Appearances matter a lot, especially in the world of business. Would you trust someone who looks shabby? Or would you want to trust someone who presents well? In reality, people who put effort into looking good appear more professional and command the respect of their work peers. This is because a well-put-together appearance projects a sense of authority, which makes people more inclined to listen to them and follow their lead. Investing in a new suit, a new pair of shoes, or even a hairstyle can instantly make you feel better, and when you feel better about yourself, you will automatically feel more confident. That said, remember that this isn't a onetime trick and that you will need to be consistent if you want to project confidence and earn the admiration of your collaborators.

Along with this, focus on developing healthy and positive body language. For starters, adopting an upright posture and maintaining eye contact is a great way to project confidence. Using a firm handshake has also been shown to be a trait of highly confident people, whether they are employees or managers. Lastly, smile. Smiling is inherently contagious in that people will mirror your attitude, which will make them more likely to trust and follow you. Initially, all this might feel a little forced. However, if you adopt these confidence tips, you'll get used to them. This is how habits are formed, and you can use the same logic to improve your confidence levels as well.

Ask for Support

A common notion has it is that asking for help makes people weak or incapable. In reality, the opposite is true. Asking for help requires a lot of courage and confidence. It takes a lot to accept that you are not good enough at something or that you need help. Do not hesitate to ask when you need help. All confident leaders do this. You can draw on someone else's talent without putting yourself down or feeling threatened. When others see you ask for help, it will instil confidence in them, too, and inspire them to do better. It also shows them it's perfectly okay to ask for help. After all, unless you ask for it, you will never get it. The next time you are feeling hesitant, ask yourself what you stand to lose by seeking help, and take the risk. It will be worth it.

Role Model

Is there a specific leader who inspires you? A role model you aspire to become. Whether it is within your organisation, your immediate superior, or someone you know or even don't know, they can be your role models. That person will be a source of inspiration and allow you to gain some much-needed confidence and wisdom. Whether they are an industry leader or charismatic public figures, it always helps to have someone to look up to. Focus on studying their behaviour, communication style, and body language. Understand how they do their thing. What are the different attributes they possess that attract you to them? Do you have any of these qualities, and if you do, how can you build upon them? Even by simply looking at, observing, and mimicking someone else's behaviour, you can significantly improve your confidence levels.

Good Network

Another simple yet effective means to build your confidence levels is networking. Network with other managers and pick those who can become powerful or useful contacts. How can you meet such people? Find out if any mutual contacts can introduce you. However, before you meet them, make sure you do some legwork about your new contact. Know how you can be of use to them, not just what you can achieve from them. This is how thriving and helpful networking works.

When you have support or even a network or a group of peers who are sailing in the same boat as you, it automatically becomes a source of strength. When you know you are not alone in the challenges you are facing, you will feel better. There is strength in numbers. You can also use this network to help deal with any challenges or problems you are facing. If you are going through something common, chances are someone somewhere has dealt with it. Getting in touch with such people automatically creates a dependable support network. In a similar fashion, be ready for people to approach you and establish a mutually beneficial connection with you.

Comfort Zone

If you want to grow as a manager, then you need to step outside your comfort zone. Staying in this zone is quite tempting. Once you are there, your motivation to step outside will be low. Unless you push yourself, you cannot become better. Focus on doing something that is beyond the scope of everything you've done so far. This is how you learn, and even children know that learning is needed for growth. Even if it is something as simple as fixing a meeting with a prominent person in your industry, go ahead and do it. Learn something new and do not become complacent at any stage. If this makes you a little uneasy, it is a good feeling. Capitalise on this and push yourself. By stretching your boundaries, you are growing, which will do wonders for your sense of confidence.

Celebrate the Wins

We are our worst critics. It is easy to be hard on yourself when things don't go your way. In reality, this is bound to happen at one point or another. However, there isn't any space for modesty in the world of business or management. You cannot become confident if you don't acknowledge your wins. Whether it is big or small, acknowledge the things you do well. Every win of yours should be celebrated. This will promote a collaborative work atmosphere conducive to wellbeing, making yourself and your collaborators feel proud and confident.

Create Opportunities

A confident manager always allows their team to grow and prosper. In that optic, allow them to make a few decisions, delegate tasks, and give them responsibilities. You don't have to do everything on your own. As a manager, you shouldn't focus purely on your own development. Rather, you need to create opportunities for the growth of your collaborators as well. Even when things don't work out, or they are headed in the wrong direction, step into your managerial role and guide them. Focus on results and allow your employees to improve their skills. When you get into the habit of recognising their efforts and wins, your confidence as a manager will also improve.

Respect

The style of management you opt for matters a lot. Understand that respect is everything. An abrasive form of leadership based on the notions of subordination and absolute control is unhelpful. Even if you get things done, it can cause discord in the team. This attitude will not earn you respect. In fact, it promotes a culture where employees only do what is asked of them and nothing more. If you want to instil a harmonious work culture, then earn your collaborators' respect. Avoid micromanaging and focus on efficient delegation. When your team can achieve the goals set for them and perform well, it will improve your self-confidence as a manager. Respect is a two-way street. It cannot be demanded and must be earned.

CHAPTER 9: PROBLEM-SOLVING

An important aspect of any professional occupation is learning about new things and gaining skills. Learning is good until a situation arises that interferes with the learning process itself. These types of situations are usually referred to as problems. While we all face problems daily, learning to cope with them is what differentiates us between those who are successful and those who are not. Some are naturally adept at problem-solving, whereas others are not, and most people are usually somewhere in between. The good news is that, as with any other skill in life, you can also learn how to solve any issue you may face. This chapter provides a comprehensive roadmap for sharpening your problem-solving skills in the context of your professional life and beyond. With all the knowledge and methods included here, you will be able to successfully and confidently rise to any challenge you will encounter on a regular basis.

Steps to Follow

Any situation that impedes achieving the goals you have set for yourself makes up a problem or roadblock. Whether it is financial, professional, or personal, we all have different goals. However, the route to achieving them is rarely straightforward. Problems can crop up at any point, anywhere, and in any activity. Without the right problem-solving skills, you cannot achieve your goals. As a manager, you must be adept at problem-solving because your team is counting on you. Invariably, your ability to deal with problems is defined by your capacity to think of solutions. Follow these simple steps for solving problems.

Step 1: Understand

A problem cannot be truly solved unless you understand what caused it. If not, the problem will probably repeat itself. So identifying the root or the primary trigger is the first step of the process. Try to understand how the domino effect created by it impedes your organisation's level of performance and goals. By zeroing in on the affected areas, it becomes easier to identify the solution. Just as with decision-making, you must have as much information regarding the problem as possible in order to fix it and ensure it doesn't appear again in the future.

Step 2: Brainstorm

After you have identified the problem and its causes or triggers, it is time to brainstorm for solutions. To do this, you will need to adapt your thinking. After all, problems cannot be solved by using the same thinking that resulted in their creation. Focus on creating a framework that will help your team tackle the problem and prevent it from repeating. Brainstorming can be done by yourself, along with your team, or both, depending on its intensity and scope and your management style. The idea of brainstorming is to come up with different solutions that can tackle and resolve the problem.

Step 3: Evaluate

Now, it is time to evaluate all the different options you have come up with in the previous step. Even if there are just two solutions to choose between, one will probably be better than the other. A brainstorming session at this stage also helps you decide what will work better for your team. It will improve their overall efficiency as well, in the sense that decisions must often be made under limited time constraints. When you are discussing and deciding the best course of action with your team, you can get helpful perspectives from them.

Step 4: Implement

The final and perhaps most crucial step is implementation. Without it, there is no point in going through the previous steps. Before implementing a particular solution, take some time to thoroughly scrutinise it to ensure there aren't any loopholes left or created by it. Make sure you consider all aspects of the decision in terms of resources for future prospects for growth. After implementation, decide if the solution creates more problems than it solves. If yes, then you'll need to think it through again. In parallel, you'll need to monitor the status of the solution after pushing through. If it doesn't work well, revisit the previous steps and implement another solution. Again, don't be shy to ask your collaborators' help so you can benefit from their direct input.

Problem-Solving Skills Managers Need

To follow the different steps mentioned above, you need some basic problem-solving skills. Here are some pointers that will come in handy.

Open Mindset

It is important to remember that a problem isn't synonymous with failure. Instead, it is merely an opportunity to learn and grow. You must keep an open mind and not be a defeatist. The cause of the problem you are dealing with might be something other than what you believe. Without an open mindset, accepting a different perspective becomes difficult. This also gives you a variety of options for possible solutions or answers. Keeping an open mindset with no biases helps you observe and notice different things that are going on, which ultimately influences your ability to achieve goals.

Attitude Matters

As with your mindset, solving a problem without the right attitude is not the right approach. You cannot tackle a problem unless you are fully aware of what has caused the situation at hand. In that regard, a positive attitude makes it easier to accept how the situation came to be and how the solutions can be implemented. While trying to solve problems, refrain from panicking, which only irritates the situation and wastes your time. Keep calm and think about a realistic and pragmatic solution. Remember that, during this situation, your team is counting on you. You cannot be an exemplary leader to them without being confident, optimistic, and positive. This also ensures the team morale doesn't plummet.

Be Analytical

Analytical skills are essential for any efficient problem solver. You'll have to be patient and carefully observe everything that goes on within your team and in the organisation. Your ability to tackle problems with facts and greater authority becomes easier with time and practice. Analytical skills also help widen the scope of skills you have already acquired.

The Questions Are Important

Humans are naturally curious, and it is time to hone your innate curiosity. A simple way to do this is by asking questions. Questions are important because asking the right ones helps identify the cause of the problem. It also offers the needed insights to quickly solve any problems you're facing. Asking the right questions and making a habit of it is the best way to go about this. The more questions you ask, the better you get at asking the right ones. Don't hesitate when you have a doubt or need to know more about a particular aspect of the situation. It's better to always ask than to work under false assumptions, which may exasperate the problem you are actively working on solving.

Be Creative

Another important skill that will help improve your problem-solving abilities is creativity. This is one skill that everyone needs. Problem-solving becomes easier because creative thinkers do not restrict themselves to a fixed framework or thinking pattern. Instead, they can think outside the box. This is not a simple thing to do, but gradually, you can get better at it. The possibilities are endless once you tap into your creative potential. A few ways to cultivate your creativity are by engaging in activities that solicit your self-expression and exposing yourself to arts, crafts, and reading. This can be performed either individually or in groups. Whichever route you decide to take to develop your creativity, you will improve your organisation, quick thinking, and problem-solving skills.

CHAPTER 10: MEANINGFUL PRODUCTIVITY

The success of any organisation or company depends on its employees and their performance. In this regard, the role of a manager cannot be overlooked. Without effective management, productivity cannot be improved. Think of it like a football team. The team will not be victorious regardless of how skilled the players are unless the coach knows how to mobilise everyone's skills. Before you can focus on improving your team's productivity, you need to concentrate on improving your own. After all, leading by example should be your motto.

To take things one step further, one of your primary goals as an efficient manager is to focus on meeting productivity. This well-known concept in the managerial world refers to one's ability to assign and carry out tasks that promote optimal utilisation of resources and maximise the results obtained. In other words, rather than implement a work methodology that is based on what's quickest or most cost-effective, meaningful productivity implies smart and sustainable work practices that will employ resources in the most efficient manner possible.

Regardless of the type of organisation you are in, here are some simple suggestions that can improve productivity.

Start with Planning

If you want to improve your productivity, then you need to plan. As you know, failing to plan is planning to fail. If you don't plan, how do you know what needs to be done or the best way to do it? Instead of going about your day haphazardly, wasting precious resources on unimportant or unnecessary tasks, concentrate on important ones. Every morning, make a list of tasks that need to be accomplished for that day. Consider the level of complexity of each of these tasks and mark them according to their priority.

While planning, focus on your energy levels throughout the day as well. There will be times when you are more energetic and resourceful than others. Schedule important and meaningful activities during your peak energy hours. For instance, if you are energetic during the morning, any task that requires proper concentration, intellectual thinking, strategic planning, and so on can be scheduled then. Similarly, any task that doesn't require much thought process or can be performed on autopilot must be scheduled for when your energy is relatively low. Your energy levels are not constant, meaning they may change now and then depending on your workload, your state of mind, how much stress you are under, etc. Be that as it may, it helps to follow a predetermined schedule to know when to tackle certain tasks in priority.

Stand-Up Meetings

Meetings are a central pillar of any business or operation. However, simply thinking about this commitment can be downright boring and tiring. It can also result in the wastage of one of the most important resources, which is time. Also, more meetings are not synonymous with better productivity. In fact, it can reduce an entire team's or department's productivity. This is one reason more and more organisations are opting for a culture that revolves around productive meetings. It involves meetings that are performed while walking or even standing. Instead of traditional ones where everyone sits around a table and listens with little contribution, opt for stand-up meetings. As the name suggests, it simply refers to a meeting format where everyone is standing. Since standing for prolonged periods is not comfortable, the meeting will end quickly. This means important information will be conveyed effectively and efficiently without wasting time. Not only will it bring down stern hierarchical barriers, but it will also bolster your productivity and that of your team.

Online Teams

When your team works remotely, it's often hard to find the right balance that can bring everyone together and keep them working as one productive unit. From different time zones to miscommunication, problems that normally don't pop up in a physical workspace can creep up on you when you least expect it. One thing that's very important is to make sure there is always an environment of inclusion in your workspace. If you're using software like Slack (and if you're not, we advise you do), it's important to keep general channels and discords active. Make everyone feel like they're heard and that their input is appreciated. Make sure you also find a comfortable way to set meetings that don't force any one member to make massive compromises to be online. Keep time zones in mind, and if that isn't helping, then dividing your team into smaller units accordingly can help. That way, everyone feels like they're heard and that they're part of the bigger picture. Do that and watch your productivity grow!

Organise Tasks

Before you focus on improving your productivity, you must understand all the different tasks, roles, and responsibilities you need to fulfil. They will be of varying importance and urgency and have different conditions and criteria. Carefully sort the tasks into different categories based on the degree of their importance and urgency. For instance, the first category will contain important and urgent tasks. The second contains tasks that are important but not urgent. The third category contains tasks that are urgent but are not important. Finally, the fourth category includes all tasks that are neither important nor urgent. Any task that falls in the fourth category should be automatically eliminated because it does not contribute to maximising productivity. Start by tackling activities that fit the first category, then move on to the second and then the third. This ensures you are getting more things done in less time and focusing on optimal resource utilisation.

Clear Goals

You cannot improve your productivity unless you are clear about the goals you wish to achieve. If you don't want to squander precious resources, then you need well-formulated goals and objectives. Setting goals is not all that difficult. You can do it easily by referring to earlier chapters and following the suggestions discussed there. However, it is not just about establishing goals. Goals and a detailed action plan will act as a roadmap to achieving them. This also ensures you don't lose sight of them and are on the right track.

Consistency

A lack of consistency is one of the common reasons for hampered productivity in the workplace. Unless you make it a habit of becoming consciously productive, you cannot achieve your goals. It's not about doing things once in a while or only when you feel like it. Instead, you need to make productivity a habit and routine. Without persistence and consistency, change isn't possible. Even if you bring about a change, it will not be sustainable. This is quite similar to how athletes' performance reduces when they stop exercising. You will need to do the same for improved, meaningful productivity.

CHAPTER 11: ADAPTABILITY

In recent years, the concept of the workplace has transformed. This means managers need to keep changing their ways, too. Your competitiveness as a manager grows when you can adapt to change in the environment at work, along with work processes. Focusing on honing your adaptability skills improves your openness and willingness to learn new skills, makes it a pleasure to face new challenges, and grants you the motivation to make adjustments whenever needed. When you are adaptable, it allows you to develop important skills, such as interpersonal skills and communication. But what does adaptability mean? It essentially refers to your ability to be flexible enough to adjust to changing conditions, your environment, and external factors. Since industry, business, and life are unpredictable, being adaptable is a highly valuable and sought-after skill.

Adaptability skills are the distinct qualities that make it possible for you to adjust quickly to any changes in the immediate environment. Whether it's your ability to quickly respond to changing roles and responsibilities, expectations and ideas, and strategies and other processes, adaptability is not restricted to just the workspace. Without it in your personal life, the chances of getting stuck increase. You also need it to promote creative thinking. So, if you want to become more adaptable and flexible as a manager, here are some suggestions that will come in handy.

Focus on the Results

Regardless of the organisation structure, you need to be more adaptable and flexible. This means you should not just focus on how the work is done, but concentrate on the results as well. It is easy to micromanage, especially when you are a manager. Most managers do it. They are used to closely observing, controlling, and reminding their subordinates about the work that needs to be done. When you stop, it increases productivity and reduces the stress others around us feel. Whether it is at work or at home, avoid micromanaging. Once you have given the responsibility of completing a task to someone else, step back and let them do it. Step in only when they ask you, or you believe certain changes are needed. In doing so, you can focus on things that require your time and attention instead of everything else.

Be Aware of the Changes

A simple yet effective way to focus on improving your adaptability skills is to manage all the changes taking place around you. This comes with assertion and mindfulness. Instead of sticking to a plan of action you have created, be aware of the changes going on. Whether it is a change in your team's budget or the work environment, stay updated about it. When anything changes, your responsibility and role will also change. Unless you are aware of such changes, you cannot adapt.

Develop a Growth Mindset

Adaptability comes with a willingness to learn and try new things. If you refuse to do this, you cannot move ahead. You need this in your personal and professional life. By developing a growth mindset, your ability to face challenges improves. Instead of being fixated on the results you are getting, you can focus on the learning involved in the process. This makes you more aware of any opportunities as well as challenges coming your way. When you are better equipped to deal with them, you can adapt quickly. Also, showing a willingness to grow by focusing on learning and developing new skills sets a good example for others to follow.

Set Goals for Yourself

To develop your adaptability skills, concentrate on setting SMART goals for yourself. The steps for this were introduced in the previous chapters. The tendency to procrastinate increases when you are facing challenging circumstances. In such instances, instead of shying away from the challenge, force yourself to face it head-on. This not only reduces the odds of procrastinating, but ensures that you are moving ahead. This, by itself, grants you the required motivation needed to move on. It also improves your ability to adapt to any changes.

Seek Feedback

Never hesitate to ask for feedback. This is essential because we all have different perspectives and ideas about how things should be done. When you ask for feedback, you will retrieve varying perspectives. Not everything will be good, and some of it will point to a need for improvement. Regardless of the feedback you receive, make sure you take it in stride. Acknowledgements help prepare you to become flexible enough in the face of changing circumstances. When you are willing to accept change, it makes you more aware of all the needed adjustments for a smoother transition. In the end, this makes it easier to deal with the changes.

Acknowledge and Accept Change

Acceptance is impossible without acknowledgement. So, if you want to become flexible, then you need to acknowledge the changes that are taking place. Learning to accept the changes is an effective step toward recognising the adjustments needed to be made. Whenever you are facing a change, acknowledge that it is taking place. The sooner you do this, the easier it is to address and accept it. If you keep shying away from it, the change will itself seem like an overwhelming challenge.

Emotional Intelligence

An important aspect of self-management skills is to focus on exercising emotional intelligence. It refers to the steps followed to control and filter your emotions in a desirable, constructive, and positive way. When you exercise emotional intelligence, instead of letting your emotions guide you, decisions come from a place of sound reason and logic. Whether you need to work with a new team or become accustomed to a new process, emotional intelligence makes such changes easier.

CHAPTER 12: CONSCIENTIOUSNESS

Do you want to improve your ability to stay organised and complete tricky tasks? Do you want to feel more connected to not just your peers, but to your job as well? If the answer is yes, then you need to become conscientious. It refers to the quality of being thoughtful, careful, and thorough. This is one of the most important personality traits a person can possess. Individuals with a high level of conscientiousness are not only aware of their actions, but the effect their actions have on others. They also feel a sense of duty towards those around them. They are extremely diligent in their work, always do their best, take their obligations seriously, and stick to regulations. Common traits associated with conscientiousness include reliability, good work ethic, punctuality, and organisation. In this section, we'll explore some steps that can be taken to become more conscientious in all aspects of your life.

Reliability

Practising the different management tactics you were introduced to previously, coupled with completing your work on time, will make you more dependable. If you maintain a good quality of work and are actively communicating with those around you, it also becomes easier to get things done. You need to become aware of how the quality of work you do ultimately influences the organisation. It also comes with the awareness that your job affects not only you, but those around you as well. So, putting your best foot forward is not simply good for advancing your career, but also for improving the lives of others around you. It is not always possible to follow plans or get the results you desire. When a problem arises, a conscientious manager will immediately and actively communicate the developments with their team members. This shows others they can count on you for reliable information.

Good Work Ethic

Having a good work ethic is essential for achieving your goals and getting things done. It also sets a good example for others to follow. There is no replacement for strong work ethics. You can improve this by fully focusing on one task at a time, efficient time management, and planning the execution to tackle difficult or complex tasks. By eliminating distractions, you can focus on making meaningful progress that enables you to do a thorough job. Whether it is getting rid of distractions, organising your workday, or taking regular breaks throughout the day, these are all simple ways to show a good work ethic. Doing this is also needed to improve your productivity at work and to strike a good work-life balance.

Organisation is Key

The importance of an organisation cannot be overstated. We have different things to do, responsibilities to fulfil, and roles to play. While doing all this, getting off track or distracted is quite common. Unless you are organised, you cannot effectively do your job. The simplest ways to improve your organisation abilities include planning your day, making a to-do list, keeping an organised workspace, and scheduling time for specific activities. These are simple yet effective techniques to improve your organisational abilities. When you're fully conscious of everything that needs to be prioritised on a daily basis and are aware of the time it will take, making significant progress becomes easier. It also allows you to avoid distractions.

Punctuality

Time is a precious commodity. Whether it is yours or someone else's, wasting it is detrimental to progress. The simplest way to foster punctuality is by being on time for meetings, meeting deadlines and obligations, and setting reminders for any upcoming deadlines. Practising punctuality is incredibly simple. Once you become punctual, you'll understand the real value of time. It gives you more control over what you are doing and how you spend your days. Practising punctuality not only shows how professional you are but also conveys a message that you value others' time as much as your own.

Perception

When you believe that what you are doing is important, enjoyable, and aligns with your core values, shifting your behaviours for the better becomes easy. Regardless of what the task is, do it wholeheartedly and do it to the best of your abilities. This is how you can improve the quality of your performance. It also helps highlight a good work ethic. In every situation, your perception matters because it ultimately guides your actions and behaviours. By maintaining an optimistic outlook, it becomes easier to get things done and carry them out properly.

Realistic Goals

Setting realistic goals is a great way to develop conscientiousness. While establishing realistic goals, visualise how you plan to achieve them and then make a note of all the steps to be followed. After this, consider any obstacles or challenges you might face. As you do this, you are becoming more conscious because it involves mindfully considering where your time and energy are to be spent. If the path to achieving a goal seems challenging, you will have an opportunity to re-evaluate how you can get to the endpoint before you get started. By doing this, you can prepare yourself and improve the overall results, too.

Better Relationships

Relationships are important in all aspects of life, and your work is not an exception. By building stronger, more meaningful relationships with your colleagues and peers, you can become more conscientious. This involves interacting with them not just regularly, but also positively. Make sure you are an active listener and pay attention to how you communicate. Focus on expressing your thoughts effectively and efficiently, with no ambiguity. Simple questions about how the other person is doing and if they need any help, can also do the trick. You don't have to go out of your way to make this effort. Instead, it is about showcasing a little mindfulness.

CHAPTER 13: DEVELOP SELF-MANAGEMENT SKILLS

So far, you have been introduced to the different types of self-management skills managers must have and how you can develop them. Following the information provided until now, your overall productivity, ability to stay organised, and sense of responsibility will improve. However, there is a difference between knowing what you should do and then deliberately practising the skills associated with self-management. In this chapter, you will be introduced to simple steps that can be implemented in your daily life to develop and improve your management skills. You will also learn how to utilise these skills in the workplace.

Tips to Improve Self-Management Skills

The wonderful thing about life is that you do not have to be content with how things are. You always have the power to change and become better. By improving your self-management skills, you can unlock your true potential. It will also teach you to be the best manager you can be.

Take Care

When you don't feel like your best self, the chances of losing your time, becoming unorganised, and losing sight of your goals increases; by prioritising your sense of wellbeing, you will have better control over your thoughts, behaviours, and actions. The simplest form of self-care involves consuming healthy and well-balanced meals, getting sufficient rest at night, efficient stress management, and engaging in regular physical activity. Once you take care of your physical health, your mental and emotional wellbeing improves. Ultimately, making a habit of this will work wonders for your workplace productivity.

Be Patient

Patience is a lost trait these days. Most of us look for instant results or gratification. Understand that not everything in life is instant. Things that matter usually take a great deal of time, effort, and commitment. Such goals cannot be accomplished overnight. In the meantime, if you lose patience, you will not reach your desired destination. Also, your ability to manage yourself improves when you learn to be patient. Be patient not just with others but with yourself, too.

One Task at a Time

An incredible way to improve your productivity while focusing on self-management is by concentrating on only one task at a time. Even if there are multiple things you want to do, start with one task. Once you have accomplished it, you can move on to the next one. If you try to do multiple things at once, chances are you will get nothing done. Even if you manage to do it, the quality of the results generated will be low. Moreover, multitasking increases the feeling of being overwhelmed and stressed. Instead, create an organisational system that works for you using the suggestions discussed in the previous chapters.

Focus on Your Strengths

Take some time for self-reflection and think about the things that you do well. Understand what you are good at and get better in those areas. By improving your strengths, you will feel better about yourself. It also gives you a better sense of control. Along with that, it unlocks your true potential. Learning to focus on your strength also makes you feel more confident and improves your self-esteem. A combination of these factors will automatically make you feel better about yourself and life in general.

Be Satisfied

Regardless of where you come from or where you want to go, you only have 24 hours at your disposal. Understand that you cannot be 100% productive every moment of the day. It's also impossible to fully stick to a schedule at all times. This is perfectly okay. Give yourself some time to relax and recharge your batteries. Instead of chasing perfection, learn to be satisfied with yourself. When your sense of self-satisfaction improves, your ability to get things done also improves. At the end of the day, avoid beating yourself up. If you want to feel satisfied, then understand that it is your decision and that no one else can do it for you. Once you learn to be satisfied with yourself, you'll stop chasing perfection and will instead concentrate on all the things that you can do. Avoid worrying about things that cannot be controlled. Instead, focus on doing your best. Even if you fall short, try the next day again, and do not call it quits.

The 2-Minute Rule

A simple yet effective means to get things done is to follow the 2-minute rule. This rule has different formats, but it's used for improving overall productivity and accountability. The rule states that if something can be completed within 2 minutes, then you should do it right away. If the task takes longer than 2 minutes, then make a note of it and add it to your list of tasks to be completed. For instance, if you think you can organise your desk in two minutes, then do it. This is a productive task. When your desk is organised, your ability to focus and concentrate improves. It also reduces physical clutter, which makes it easier to work. Instead of putting this simple task on hold, you are doing it without delay, which brings you a sense of accomplishment.

Be Consistent

Remember that life is not a sprint, but a marathon. Therefore, it's not just about starting strong, but also your ability to maintain this momentum throughout. You don't have to utilise all your energy and resources in a single day. Instead, plan such that you can make the most of the resources and time available at your disposal. Instead of focusing on random bursts of energy, make a little progress every day. Even making a 1% change and improvement daily will result in a massive change by the end of the year. This is what consistency is about. If you can consistently stick to working on your goals and focus on improving your self-management skills, you will eventually get there.

How to Use Self-Management Skills

An important aspect of self-management is regulating your actions. Others will view you as a respectable and professional employee when you can regulate your actions and put your best foot forward. Here are some simple suggestions for practising efficient self-management at the workplace.

Establish Goals

The idea behind effective management is to reach your professional goals and ambitions. By setting your goals and staying on track, you can achieve this. When you are on the right track and measure your progress, it shows that you are good at managing your time and priorities. While setting goals, don't forget to go through all the various suggestions discussed in the previous chapters.

Start Planning

It's not just about establishing long- or short-term goals for yourself. Instead, you need to plan all your workdays. Make it a point to keep a calendar or anything else that promotes a better organisation. Write down all the different tasks and then start prioritising when the time comes to complete them. Also, ensure that you regularly check the plan you have made to prevent wasting resources. When your workdays are well chalked out, the chances of getting distracted or deviating from the goals reduce. This will improve your productivity and show others how they're supposed to achieve their goals and practice self-management for themselves.

Be Prepared

Conducting and attending meetings is an important aspect of your job as a manager. Therefore, you must always be prepared before meetings. An unfruitful meeting not only wastes your time, but those of others as well. A simple means to show others that you have self-control is by being prepared before meetings. This means that before heading over to a meeting, you do a little research and organise your notes. Have a few meaningful talking points and gather the required information. Ensure that you are always on time or early (but never so early that you waste your own time) for a meeting and are never late. After all, as a manager, others look up to you. Therefore, you need to lead by example.

Always Think

A common thing most of us do is speak without giving it much thought. Remember, words are incredibly powerful. They can have a positive or negative impact depending on how or when you say them. If you take a moment and think things through before speaking, the chances of unknowingly hurting someone else reduce. It also makes the workplace more peaceful and conducive to growth. Even if you are offering feedback to your employees, there is no reason to be harsh. Everything can be said in a positive and constructive manner. There is no space for negativity in the workspace, so make it a habit of pausing and thinking before saying something. Other than in the workplace, being a thoughtful and strategic communicator will benefit you in all aspects of your personal and social life.

PART B: ALL ABOUT TIME MANAGEMENT

Your quality of life, to a significant extent, is defined by how you think and feel about yourself. Self-esteem is the emotional core of your overall personality. How much you like yourself and how you live your life is determined by this. It is influenced by how you utilise the time available at your disposal and your life in general to enhance your overall potential. When you work efficiently, your self-esteem increases and vice versa. Self-efficacy is the other side of the coin. It refers to the extent to which you feel competent, productive, and capable. It also includes how you feel about your ability to solve problems, complete your work, and achieve any established goals. Your self-esteem improves when you feel capable, competent, and productive. Those who manage their time properly and confidently always feel in control of their lives.

Before moving on to the different concepts of time management to make the most of the time available at your disposal, it is important to understand psychology. The psychology of time management is based on a simple concept known as the law of control. It essentially states that the extent to which you feel good about yourself is the same as the extent to which you feel that you have a hold on your life. When you start to feel that that hold on your life, work, or any other aspect starts to slip away, it triggers negative feelings about yourself. This causes a difference between the internal and external loci of control. An internal locus makes you feel you are the master of your destiny. Whereas an external locus is about feeling that external forces or circumstances are regulating your life.

If your locus is external, then you might feel that your boss, the bills you have to pay, or any other stress of work and life is controlling you. It might make you feel as if there is a lot that you need to do within an extremely short frame of time. This can make you feel that you're not in charge of your life, let alone your time. This is precisely what most of us are guilty of doing. Hour after hour and day after day, we are unknowingly giving away our sense of control to external sources that are beyond our scope of control.

You need to understand that there is a significant gap between self-determined action and a reaction that is primarily a response to an external stressor. This is the difference between feeling in control of your life and being optimistic and feeling stressed, pressured, and extremely negative about yourself and life. If you want to do your best, then you need to feel in control of your life. After all, it is your life, and you are the only one living it.

We have an internal program responsible for regulating our behaviours and important aspects of life. This is known as self-concept. Those with a high self-concept view themselves as well-organised and productive, especially in terms of time management. They believe they are in charge of their lives and time. All the different ideas, images, and beliefs you hold about yourself determine your self-concept. It's also influenced by your ability to manage the time available. They are efficient and well-organised. On the other hand, some constantly feel overwhelmed by their circumstances and the surrounding people. Even if you feel the latter, it can be changed.

Take a minute and ask yourself what you believe about yourself, as well as your time management capabilities. Do you think you are efficient with your time management? Do you believe you are in control of your life and how you spend your time? Regardless of what you believe, if you think you are an excellent time manager, then your beliefs will be consistent with them. This is because your inherent self-concept by itself pushes you to focus on consistency between the individual you are and how you perform on the outside. Before you learn about different things you can do to become good at time management, it's important to understand that you need to keep a positive mindset. If you think you can become good, then you will. If you think you will never be good, then getting out of that hard place becomes difficult. Unless you are willing to change certain beliefs about yourself, you cannot improve, learn, or grow.

The next aspect that you need to concentrate on is deciding. A decision should be about how you think you can develop positive and helpful beliefs, not just about yourself but your personal productivity, too. The good news is that making this decision is not difficult. You need to follow the concept of the four Ds. The four Ds refer to desire, decisiveness, determination, and discipline. You will need to consciously decide to develop helpful time management habits. Whether it is ensuring that you are always on time for a meeting or establishing strict timelines for completing a task, these are some habits you can develop. Without this conscious decision, you cannot make the needed change.

After you have decided that you want to become a highly productive manager, you will need to program your mind for it. The first aspect of doing this is to focus on your inner dialogue. If you take a moment, you will realise there is an internal dialogue that's constantly going on in the back of your mind. How you talk to yourself is incredibly important. It is also known as self-talk. Self-talk has a significant effect on your behaviours, actions, and even thoughts and beliefs. If it is negative, everything else takes on a negative colour. If you keep thinking that you are a highly productive person and manage your time efficiently, then your actions, behaviours, and thoughts will be directed such that this internal dialogue is strengthened. On the other hand, if you think you are highly unorganised or cannot manage your time properly, it will become a self-fulfilling prophecy.

Before moving on to all the different steps, you can follow to manage time properly. Another technique that can program your mind is visualisation. It's an incredibly simple yet effective technique. All you need to do is find a quiet space for yourself, sit with your eyes closed, and visualise how your life will be once you learn to manage your time effectively and efficiently. The visualisation in your head will create an image of a person who is in control of not just themselves but their life, too. If this visualisation appeals to you, understand that you have the power to turn it into a reality. The person who you see on the inside is the person you will become on the outside. This is how powerful visualisation is. Even if you are a highly productive person, do you think there's something else you can do better? Do you believe there is further scope for improvement in learning? If yes, think how much better you will feel about yourself as well as your life once you make some changes. You'll be relaxed, composed, in control, and confident at all times. Doesn't that create a strikingly wonderful version of reality?

Well, use the different suggestions given in this part of the book to achieve this.

Along with monitoring your self-talk and visualisation, there is another technique that can reprogram your mind to become an efficient time manager. This is known as the "As if" method. This is quite similar to the visualisation method. Instead of just visualising, you'll need to behave and act as if you are already an efficient time manager. This is an excellent way to develop healthy and desirable behaviours. If you were good at managing your time, how would you behave? What are the things that you will do differently? Think about this and start projecting the same. For instance, if you think that you'll be spending more time with your family or will achieve a work-life balance once you manage time, it is time to do it immediately. Even if you don't think you are good at it, if you pretend or behave like your actions themselves generate positive feelings, they will improve your personal efficiency; when you can see the results for yourself, the motivation and inclination to make the change become easier.

CHAPTER 14: TIME MANAGEMENT CHALLENGES

We all face time management challenges in our lives. Whether we're trying to juggle a full-time job, school, family, or social life, or we're simply trying to make the most of our free time, we can all benefit from learning how to manage our time more effectively. Not only can it help us become more productive, but it can also reduce stress and help us enjoy our lives more.

This chapter will discuss some of the most common challenges we face and offer tips on how to overcome them. We'll also dispel some common myths about managing time and discuss some of the most common obstacles to effective time management. Finally, we'll provide some tips on how to make it a habit.

Dealing with Time Constraints

Time management is an important skill for anyone who wants to be successful in today's fast-paced world. Learning to make the most of the time you have available can help you achieve your goals, both personal and professional. Of course, managing your time is not always easy, and there will always be times when you feel you're up against the clock. However, some strategies can help you deal with time constraints and make the most of your time.

By taking small steps, you can ensure that you're making progress without feeling overwhelmed. In addition, it's crucial to be flexible and willing to adjust your plans as needed. You can learn to manage your time more effectively by following these tips.

Setting Priorities

Time management is a skill that can be difficult to master, but it's important to learn how to set priorities to make the most of the time you have. One way to do this is to keep a list of tasks that need to be completed and then rank them in order of importance. It can also be helpful to set deadlines for yourself and to break down larger projects into smaller goals that can be accomplished within a certain timeframe.

If you find yourself constantly running out of time, it might be necessary to re-evaluate your priorities and see if there are any areas where you can cut back. By learning how to set priorities, you can make the most of the time you have and get more done. The key is to find a system that works for you and stick with it.

Breaking Down Tasks

One of the biggest challenges we all face is how to deal with time constraints. Whether we're trying to get a project done at work, meet a deadline for school, or manage our daily to-do list, it's tough to stay on track when there's so much to do and so little time to do it. One of the best ways to deal with time constraints is to use the *Pomodoro Technique*. This strategy allows you to focus on one task at a time and then take a break when you need it.

By taking a big task and breaking it down into smaller steps, we can make headway without feeling overwhelmed. And once we've completed one small step, we'll have a better sense of how much time we need to complete the rest of the task. So next time you're feeling stressed about a looming deadline, remember that breaking down tasks can help you get the job done.

Managing Distractions

Time constraints are a fact of life. Whether it's meeting a deadline at work or getting the kids to soccer practice on time, we all have to deal with them daily. One of the biggest challenges in dealing with time constraints is managing distractions. Whether it's a co-worker dropping by for a chat or an unexpected phone call, distractions can quickly eat in our precious time.

The key to managing distractions is to be aware of them and have a plan for dealing with them. For example, if you know that you're going to be interrupted during a crucial part of your work, you can schedule some "buffer time" into your day so that you can still meet your deadlines. By being prepared for distractions, you can ensure that they don't take control of your day.

Staying on Track

One of the most challenging aspects of managing a project is staying on track despite time constraints. Whether you're working with a limited budget or facing a tight deadline, it's important to be efficient and keep your team focused. Here are a few tips for dealing with time constraints and staying on track.

- First, make sure you clearly understand the scope of the project and what needs to be done.
- Once you have a plan, break the work down into smaller tasks and assign them to team members.
- Establish regular checkpoints and deadlines, so everyone knows what needs to be done and when it needs to be done.
- Don't be afraid to delegate tasks and ask for help when needed.

By following these tips, you can ensure that your project stays on track despite any time constraints.

Learning to Procrastinate Productively

We've all been there before - staring at a project that seems impossible to complete in the time we have. Whether it's a school assignment, work presentation, or home improvement project, sometimes it can feel like we're up against the clock. In these situations, it's crucial to learn how to procrastinate productively.

One of the best ways to do this is to break the task down into smaller, more manageable pieces. You might not finish the entire project in one sitting, but you can probably complete one small part of it. By taking it one step at a time, you'll gradually make progress and avoid feeling overwhelmed.

It's also vital to set realistic goals. If you're constantly putting pressure on yourself to finish something by an unrealistic deadline, you're likely to end up feeling stressed and frustrated. Instead, give yourself some breathing room and allow some flexibility.

Finally, don't forget to take breaks! It's easy to get caught up in a project and lose track of time, but if you push yourself too hard, you'll just end up feeling burnt out. Take a few minutes every so often to stretch your legs, grab a snack, or take a few deep breaths. By taking care of yourself, you'll be in a better frame of mind to work on your project.

Time Management Myths

Time management is a hot topic, with many people eager to make the most of each day. Unfortunately, there are many myths out there about managing time effectively, and paying too much attention to these myths can lead to more stress and less productivity. For example, many people believe they don't have enough time to get everything done. However, time is a relative concept, and often it's simply a matter of priorities. By busting these myths, you can start managing your time in a way that works best for you. Here are a few common ones:

Myth 1: Time Management Is about Working Faster

One of the most common myths is that it's all about working faster. This couldn't be further from the truth! Proper scheduling is actually about working smarter, not harder or faster. For example, let's say you have a project that is due in two weeks. You could start working on it right away and work on it non-stop until it's due. Or, you could break the project down into smaller tasks and spread them out over the two weeks so that you're not feeling overwhelmed at the end.

This is just one example of how working smarter can help you manage your time better. Many other strategies can help you make the most of your time. So, if you're feeling bogged down by your to-do list, don't despair. There are plenty of resources available to help you get started with managing time effectively. Just remember, it's not about working harder or faster; it's about working smarter.

Myth 2: You Can't Manage Time; You Can Only Manage Yourself.

One of the most pervasive time management myths is that you can't manage time; you can only manage yourself. The implication is that time is this impersonal, inflexible force that we're all subject to, and the best we can do is try to work within its limitations. But the truth is that we can manage time; we just have to approach it in the right way. The goal is really about creating systems and structures that work for us rather than against us.

By understanding how we work best and making small tweaks to our routines, we can regain control over our time and start getting more done. So, if you feel you're always struggling to keep up with your to-do list, remember that you have the power to change that. With a bit of effort, you can start managing your time instead of feeling like it's managing you.

Myth 3: You Need to Work Long Hours to Be Successful

There's a common belief that to be successful, you need to put in long hours at work. While it's true that hard work is important, the idea that you need to work around the clock to achieve your goals is a myth. Research has shown that working excessive hours can lead to decreased productivity and lower quality of work. That's because our brains are not designed to operate at full capacity for extended periods.

Instead, we need periodic breaks to stay focused and fresh. So, if you're looking to improve your management skills, don't feel you need to sacrifice your personal life to get ahead. A healthy balance of work and free time is the key to success.

Myth 4: Multitasking Is the Key to Managing Time Effectively

One of the most popular misconceptions is that switching tasks helps you be productive. The truth is, however, that multitasking is counterproductive. When you try to do too many things at once, you end up spreading yourself thin and not doing any of them very well.

You might answer a few emails while you're on the phone, but you will not be able to give either task your full attention. As a result, it's going to take you longer to complete both tasks, and the quality of your work will suffer. If you want to be truly productive, focus on one task at a time and give it your full attention. You'll be surprised at how much faster and better you can get things done.

Myth 5: Time Management Is Only for Busy People

The idea that it's only for busy people is one of the most common misconceptions. In reality, managing time is a skill that can benefit everyone. After all, we all have the same number of hours in a day. The key is to use those hours effectively. It can help you make the most of your time so that you can accomplish your goals, both big and small. It involves setting priorities, creating a schedule, and learning to say no to distractions.

If you're not sure where to start, there are plenty of resources available to help you get started, including books, websites, and even apps. To recommend a few, try checking out the book *"The Time Trap"* by Alec Mackenzie, the website *"Time Management Ninja"*, or the app *Toggl*. So don't let this myth hold you back from achieving your goals. Try it - you might be surprised at how much it can help you accomplish.

Overcoming Common Obstacles

Many people struggle with managing their time effectively. This can lead to missed deadlines, unfinished projects, and a general sense of chaos. Fortunately, there are some simple steps you can take to overcome common obstacles.

Perfectionism

We all want to be perfect. We want to have the perfect job, the perfect partner, the perfect house, and the perfect life. Unfortunately, the quest for perfection can often lead to feelings of frustration and inadequacy. This is especially true when it comes to managing time effectively. Perfectionists often have difficulty completing tasks because they are constantly trying to find the perfect way to do things. As a result, they can spend hours or even days on a single task, only to end up feeling disappointed with the results.

If you are a perfectionist, learn to let go of your need for perfectionism. Try to focus on completing tasks rather than on doing them perfectly. Remember that often good enough is good enough. And if you make a mistake, don't worry—you can always fix it later. Recognising and overcoming your perfectionism is an important step in becoming an effective time manager.

Procrastination

Procrastination is one of the most prevalent problems. Put simply, procrastination is the act of delaying or postponing something. We all do it from time to time, but for some people, it can become a serious problem that gets in the way of achieving their goals. If you find yourself regularly putting things off, there are a few things you can do to overcome this obstacle.

First, try to identify the root cause of your procrastination. Are you avoiding something because you're worried about failing? Or are you simply overwhelmed by the task at hand? Once you know what's causing you to procrastinate, you can develop a plan to address the issue. For example, if you're worried about failing, you might set smaller goals or break the task down into more manageable steps.

If you're feeling overwhelmed, try focusing on one thing at a time or setting a timer and working for a set amount of time. Overcoming procrastination takes effort and practice, but it's possible with a bit of help.

Lack of Motivation

Time management is a skill that anyone can benefit from. However, managing time productively is not always easy. One common obstacle is a lack of motivation. It's hard to get started when you're not sure where to begin or what the end goal is. However, there are a few ways to overcome this obstacle. First, try to break down your goals into smaller steps. This will make them seem more achievable and less daunting.

Second, try to set regular reminders for yourself. Whether it's a daily To Do list or a weekly planner, seeing your tasks written down can help to give you a sense of purpose. Finally, try to find an accountability partner. This could be a friend, family member, or even a co-worker. Having someone to check in with can help to keep you on track and motivated.

While a lack of motivation can be frustrating, it doesn't have to be a roadblock. By taking small steps and being proactive, you can overcome this obstacle and start managing your time more effectively.

Making Time Management a Habit

Many people struggle with managing their time, feeling like they are always playing catch up. If this sounds familiar, there is hope. Making time management a habit can help you take control of your schedule and make the most of your time. One way to do this is to set aside some time each day to plan out your tasks. This will help you see what needs to be done and prioritise your time accordingly.

Additionally, try to break down larger projects into smaller steps that you can complete over some time. And don't forget to schedule some downtime! Allowing yourself regular breaks will help you avoid burnout and stay on track. With a little effort, you can make a great habit that sticks.

Common obstacles to managing time productively include perfectionism, procrastination, and a lack of motivation. However, these obstacles can be overcome with little effort and practice. Making time management a habit can help you take control of your schedule and make the most of your time. With a bit of planning and effort, you can achieve your goals and make the most of your time.

CHAPTER 15: STEPS FOR BETTER TIME MANAGEMENT

In this chapter, you will learn about all the different steps you can follow to manage your time effectively and efficiently.

Identify Your Values

Time management is not just restricted to a single aspect of your life. Instead, it is a way to manage your life itself. It also helps improve your productivity. However, before you can achieve this, you will need to determine your values.

If you want to manage your time properly, you need to learn to control different events and ensure they are in harmony with the things that matter the most to you. If it isn't important to you or you do not value it, chances are you will not find the motivation needed to make the change. Before you do something, ask yourself why you are doing it. For instance, if you need to wake up at a certain time, ask yourself why you need to wake up so early. If your reason isn't good enough or doesn't give you any value, you will not want to wake up on time!

The next step of this process is to determine what you value the most. To do this, here are some questions you can use.

- What is most important to me?
- What do I care about?
- What do I stand for?
- What will I not stand for?

Take some time and reflect on these questions and answer them honestly. There is no point in doing anything if you aren't honest at this stage. Once you are aware of your values, living life according to them becomes easier. In fact, your overall satisfaction and feel-good quotient also improve when you are living in sync with these values. Most of the stress, frustration, anxiety, or worry you experience in your personal or professional life is primarily because what you are doing is not in sync with your values. When what you do differs completely from what you believe in, you cannot feel good on the inside. Managers experience burnout because of the stress and pressures of their work. When you love what you are doing and the work you do is a genuine reflection of your values, you will feel better from the inside. Because of this, your ability to deal with stress also improves. This reduces the risk of burnout. So, take all the time that is needed and examine your core values, beliefs, and convictions. If you could change anything on the outside or the inside to live by these values, what would it be? Think about all this and then move on to the next step.

You need to not just realise, but acknowledge and accept the simple fact that you are a unique and amazing person the way you are. Your values are not things that have cropped up overnight. Instead, they are the ideas or basic notions by which you have lived your entire life. This can happen knowingly and unknowingly. In fact, most of us develop our values somewhere along the way. It's our life experiences and expectations, as well as different scenarios we encounter in a professional and personal capacity, that shape our values. They are a part of your emotional as well as psychological makeup. They are an integral aspect of your personality and character. For now, take the time needed to identify your innermost values.

If you are unsure of your values, here is a simple exercise that will give you some much-needed insights.

- How would you describe yourself?
- How would you describe others and people in general?
- What do you think of life?
- What is your biggest goal?

Answering these questions requires some introspection. However, take the time needed and think about them carefully. They will give you a better idea of the kind of person you are.

Vision and Mission Matter

We all think different thoughts every single day. At any given point, different ideas will swirl in your head. However, we all don't think in the same way, and therefore, different thought processes are at play. Two different types of thinking are needed to deal with different situations we face daily: fast and slow thinking. Fast thinking essentially refers to the kind needed to deal with short-term tasks, problems, activities, situations, and even responsibilities. It's about acting quickly and instinctively. This is the most appropriate form for daily activities that you can pretty much perform on autopilot. The second type, slow thinking, involves taking a step back and carefully pondering through the details before deciding what to do. Not engaging in slow thinking when needed increases the chances of making mistakes or not achieving the goals you have established. If you want to become good at managing your time, then you need to understand that you are the only one who can regulate it. You have control over your life and your time. You can do this better by engaging in slow thinking regularly. Before you do something, ask yourself, "What am I trying to do?"

You might have noticed that you are working hard but haven't taken the time needed to think about what you are trying to accomplish. Most of us have done this at some point or another. If you were driving from destination A to B but were not aware of the route, the chances of getting lost in this process are high. If you are on the wrong route, then redoubling your efforts doesn't matter because you have already forgotten the aim. This is precisely what happens if you do not engage in analysis and introspection. These are two aspects important for slow thinking. Slow thinking enables you to focus on the goals you wish to achieve and how you want to do it.

Start with the End in the Mind

You must be clear about what you desire or the result you want. If you have no clarity about what you are trying to achieve, how will you even get there? Also, all the time, energy, and resources that have been utilised so far would have gone to waste. Where do you want to end up at the end of the day? Once you learn to answer this question, you can ensure that you are working toward it. This reduces the wastage of precious resources, especially time. If you don't have a specific goal in mind, it also starts eating away at your commitment, motivation, and enthusiasm. It will leave you feeling dissatisfied and unfulfilled. When you have a big goal or an objective you wish to accomplish, it will lead you to success.

Your Methodology

Once you are fully aware of what you want to achieve, the next step is to focus on how you want to get there. How are you going to do it? By focusing on this simple question, you get valuable insights to carefully analyse the situation and determine whether you are on the right track. After this, you need to focus on the progress you are making. It's not just about the journey - you also need to measure how far you have come and the distance to be covered. Without this, the chances of getting off-track increase. When you need to do something, ask yourself whether it's moving you toward your goal. If it is, consider whether it is the most efficient way to do it. If it is not, you need to go back and reconsider what you can do to achieve your goals. This also reduces the chances of indulging in unproductive activities or tasks that don't add any value or meaning to your life.

A Better Way

While you are thinking about "How is it going?" you need to consider another important question which is whether there is a better way to do what you are doing. Almost always, there will be a different and more efficient means to get to the goal you want. If you don't consider the multiple routes available, you might end up missing out on a quick, effective, and easier available option. This is important because there are many people who are working hard, but they are not working in the right direction or are making progress in the wrong direction. Ensure that you do not fall into this category of individuals who are working hard but don't know where they want to go. They do things because they don't want to deal with the possibility of being wrong or getting caught in tough situations. By asking yourself some tough questions and following the process of slow thinking, you can make the most of the time available.

Written Plans

If you want to manage time effectively and efficiently, then you will need to become good at planning. It doesn't matter whether it's a major or minor objective, make a note of it. Simply putting down all the things you want to accomplish by itself gives you the motivation to get things done. Along with that, it gives you an idea about all that has to be completed. For instance, if a new project is in the crosshairs, take the time needed to establish what has to be accomplished. After this, make an ordered list of all the steps to be taken for project completion. Ensure that the steps are written in a proper sequence.

Even though the act of planning takes a couple of extra minutes, do it. Think of it as an investment that will repay multiple times over. Every minute that you spend planning and making a written plan, you save more during the execution stage. It also reduces the chances of making mistakes and gives you a better idea of how to overcome any challenges or hurdles you might face along the way. Once you are aware of the goal you want to achieve, it's time to make a list of all that you can think of and can do to achieve it. Keep doing this until you have completed the list and are satisfied with it. All the items on the list must be organised based on their priority and sequence.

While organising the list as per the sequence, the activities need to be stated in chronological order. You need to start with the first step and repeat this process until you have reached the last one. Even a big goal can be achieved if you break it down into parts that are small enough to be accomplished one at a time. So, regardless of how overwhelming or challenging a specific goal seems right now, by breaking it down into simple steps that are listed in chronological order, it will feel less challenging and overwhelming.

Next, you will need to prioritise the items on the list. Go with the basic notion that you must focus on activities that offer maximum value. Not all steps are equally important, and some don't need as much time as others. However, the decision will be based on their priority as per the value offered. By setting priorities, it becomes easier to focus on important tasks or activities without losing sight of them. Never let the things that matter the most to you be held at the mercy of the ones that don't matter.

It's not just about creating a plan; it must be reviewed too. Even the most well-laid-out plans can go awry. To reduce the chances of this, you need to keep reviewing and updating the plan as you go along. This is because nothing in life is fixed, and change is the only constant. The circumstances under which the plan was created can change, and the same plan might no longer be ideal. Similarly, your goal itself might change, and therefore, the plan must change too. Whenever you receive any new information or feedback, don't hesitate to change the plan as needed. The most common cause of failure is action with no planning. This activity by itself will teach you to be more patient, too.

If you want to be successful, then an important part of it is clarity. You cannot become successful unless you have total clarity about where you want to go and how you can get there. You should also have clarity about who you are and what you are trying to achieve. Along with written goals, make it a point to create plans for your daily life as well. Every day, make a list of things that you want to accomplish and ensure the plan is ideal and possible.

Here are three questions you must ask yourself after setting a goal.

1. Are there any difficulties, obstacles, or challenges that stand between you and what you wish to achieve?

2. Do you need any additional skills, knowledge, or information to achieve the goal?

3. Are there any other individuals, groups, or even organisations you can use to help you?

Take the time needed to think through these questions. Let's assume that you have a specific goal in your head. Before you get started, identify any potential obstacles or hurdles you might face. Remember, life isn't smooth sailing, and there will be trouble along the way. Anticipating and preparing for it is the best course of action available. Since challenges cannot be avoided, dealing with them becomes easier if you know what to do. This isn't possible without planning. Similarly, think through the other questions and carefully make a note of your answers.

Create To-Do Lists

One of the most powerful ways to make the most of the time available is by creating a daily list of activities. This will act as a blueprint for you. You need to think on paper and then work as per the list of activities you have made a note of. Regardless of how experienced a pilot is, they always use a checklist before taking off. This ensures they have overlooked nothing, and that everything is in order before the flight. Similarly, take a couple of minutes daily to create a list of activities you have to accomplish by the end of the day. Usually, the best time to do it is right before you go to bed. Once you have a list in place, the subconscious mind can work on how you want to accomplish the task while you sleep. So, when you wake up in the morning, you'll have some ideas about how you want to tackle the day. Ensure that the last thing you do daily is to make a list of activities you want to accomplish on the following day.

Have you ever found yourself tossing and turning at night, trying hard to remember something you need to do? Once you have a list in place and have made a note of it, your ability to sleep improves. If you get sufficient rest at night, you can function effectively and efficiently the following day. It takes barely 10 minutes to make a list of activities you want to accomplish. However, the time spent doing it will improve your overall productivity and reduce time wastage. It also ensures that you are not wasting your time and effort on unimportant tasks or any other activities that don't offer value addition.

Once you have a list of all the things you need to do on the following day, use the ABCDE method to organise your list of activities. The consequence is the most important word in time management. The importance of a task is determined by the potential consequences associated with either doing or not doing it. While establishing priorities, apply this principle for every task you have included in the list. Always start with the one that has the greatest consequence. This is where the ABCDE method steps into the picture. Each must be assigned a specific letter based on its importance or the consequences associated with doing or not doing it. All the tasks that you must do must be marked with an A next to them. Similarly, the letter B signifies all activities that you should do but have milder consequences than the previous one. Ensure that you never move on to the next label without completing all the ones labelled A. Category C includes all activities that are nice to do but barely have any consequences, regardless of whether it is positive or negative. This can involve chatting with a co-worker, checking your emails, replying to any feedback you have received, and so on. These are activities that are usually enjoyable but don't have any consequences when not done.

We are all creatures of habit. Effective people have good habits that enable them to improve their productivity. On the other hand, those who are ineffective usually have bad habits they've grown accustomed to. Most get into the habit of coming to work and engaging in activities that are of low or no value and usually result in time wastage. Whether it is reading the newspaper, getting a cup of coffee, or checking your email, such activities do not offer any value whatsoever. And they take away the time available at your disposal.

The good news is that you have the power to make and break habits. If something is eating away the time available, then replace it with a more desirable habit. If you are used to checking email as soon as you enter the workspace, avoid doing it until it becomes absolutely necessary. Engage in tackling all the tasks that are labelled as A before moving on to anything else.

Now, let us go back to the ABCDE method. Any activity that is labelled as D is something that can be delegated to others. The idea is to delegate everything that someone else can do so that you can focus only on important and priority-based activities. When your time is freed up, you can focus on the completion of important activities that determine the course of your career. Another category of activities that result in time wastage belongs to category E. This category includes activities that must be eliminated. Unless you stop doing things that are unnecessary, you cannot make the most of the time available. It's quite natural to slip into our comfort zones during our work as well as our careers. However, when you become too comfortable doing certain things, it prevents your growth and development. Instead of engaging in such activities, try to focus on others.

You will need to plan your work. And you must learn to work on your plan as well. All your lists are going to be meaningless unless you do something about them. If a new project or a task comes up, make a note of it in your to-do list and then assign it a priority as per its importance. If you don't make a note of it, then you'll end up reacting and responding to the changes instead of dealing with them effectively and efficiently. Taking a couple of extra minutes to make a note of the additional tasks reduces later. Remember, having any sort of time management system in place is so much better than not having a system altogether. These days, you have a variety of applications and online options that can be utilised for tracking what you are doing and when you are doing it.

Just like a to-do list, you should also have a not-to-do list in place. This list essentially includes all the different types of tasks and activities that you must not do, regardless of how tempting they become. This list includes a variety of distractions and menial activities that offer no productivity or return. You simply need to say no instead of focusing on activities of the highest value that represent good time management.

Saying "no" by itself is the most efficient means to save time. We are all good at wasting the time available. Whenever a distraction becomes too tempting, or you want to focus on something, you know you shouldn't ask yourself, "Is this the best way I can utilise my time?" If you answer this question honestly, you will not want to squander the time available on unnecessary activities. If your answer is no, move on and focus on the important task that you need to complete.

Prioritisation

Time management always boils down to determining the most important tasks that can be done at any given moment. The next part of it involves getting the required tools and techniques to get started with that task until it reaches a logical conclusion. In the previous section, you were introduced to the ABCDE method of establishing priorities. This is a simple yet effective technique. Along with that, several other techniques can be used for prioritising the time available. If you cannot prioritise, you will end up squandering the time available on material things.

Pareto Principle

An Italian economist named Vilfredo Pareto came up with the 80/20 rule in 1895. This rule applies to money, property, and wealth accumulation in every society. After researching, he noticed that 20% of individuals controlled about 80% of wealth and property in Europe. Pareto's rule not only applies to wealth domination but can apply to all aspects of human life, including work, especially in terms of our tasks and responsibilities. This principle states that around 20% of your efforts will typically produce 80% of the results. This is true in any situation.

Therefore, before you start a typical workday, quickly review the list, and select the 20% of tasks that amount to the highest value in the list. They are the greatest contributions you can make toward achieving important goals and objectives. Let's assume that you have ten items that must be accomplished by the end of the day. If you go through this list, you realise that only a few of these items, when put together, will be worth significantly more than all the other items bunched together. By improving your ability to identify such items, you can improve your chances of success.

Turn the Pressure On

Turning on the pressure is another technique that can improve your overall productivity. Ask yourself, if you were o go on leave for a month starting tomorrow, what is the most crucial activity you would want to accomplish before leaving? Once you are aware of this answer, start working on it before moving on to any of the other things on your list. One thing that impedes time management, as well as personal productivity, is focusing on all the minor things that you need to do. This is because humans have a natural tendency to opt for the path of least resistance. So, any task that enables you to stay or settle into a comfort zone will seem more attractive than a challenging one. Even if the challenging one is the most important, the small and easy task is enjoyable, and therefore, the chances of completing it are higher.

However, unless you get the major tasks out of the way, your productivity will not improve.

So, even if you've completed only 3 or 4 out of the 10 tasks you had to do, you would have at least completed the most important ones. Then, at the end of the day, you have still been productive, even if you didn't complete the entire to-do list. This, in turn, will improve your motivation to tackle the other tasks the following day. It also increases your sense of satisfaction.

The Law of Three

The law of three is also quite similar to the Pareto principle. It essentially refers to the simple idea that there are only three tasks or activities that you perform every month that account for 90% of your overall productivity or success. If you make a list of all the things that you accomplished in a month, you'll have a long list. It can include 30, 40, or even more tasks. However, if you carefully go through the list, you realise that only about 2 or 3 of them are of significant importance. They are the ones that account for the most value you will deliver. So, how can you determine the big three? Make a list of all your tasks and responsibilities. This list must include everything that you need to do from the first day until the last day of the month. After this, answer the questions given below, and you will have your answer.

1. If you could do only one thing on the list all day long, then which activity would offer the greatest value to your organisation and goals?

2. If you could do only two things out of the list you have created, which activity would be the second-biggest accomplishment for you and the organisation?

3. If you can do only three things on your list all day long, what will be the third biggest contribution you can make?

Take the time needed and consider these questions. If you cannot answer these questions, then you are going to be in trouble. If you don't know the answer, you'll end up wasting time and resources at your disposal too. If you don't know the answer to these questions, then you will squander time on activities of no value or extremely low value. If you need some help or insight to determine the answer, reach out to others and brainstorm.

Pass It Along

Once you are aware of your big threes, the next step is to enable all those who report to you to gain clarity about their big threes. This is one of the most generous things a manager can do for their team members. By enabling them to focus on the most important things that they can do, their contribution to the organisation also improves. This creates a highly productive and efficient team. When a department of an organisation is professionally managed, all the employees in it know exactly what the most important activities are and how they can make their greatest contribution to it. Since it is an organisation, at the end of the day, it's not just about individual employees focusing on their big threes. Instead, it's about everyone walking together to complete more of the big three tasks.

If a manager is usually focused on fast thinking, they react and responds naturally to the demands and pressures at any given moment. The chances of them veering off-track are quite high. This means that the tasks of higher priority are often forgotten about or left until it is too late. Ensure that this is not a practice you get into. Take the time needed to slowly think things through before taking a step. Every moment you spend planning before taking a step will save time later.

The most important question you need to focus on in time management is, "What is the most valuable application of my time right now?" You will need to ask this question over and over until it becomes a habitual thought process. Unless you can effectively identify and answer this at every moment, you cannot focus on the most important activities. The answer to this question will guide and motivate you to focus on tasks of the highest value or important activities. When all the time available is organised on activities associated with this answer, you'll be astonished at how productive you can truly be.

According to you, what is your most valuable financial asset? Chances are, different things come to your mind, like property, jewellery, or something else along these lines. However, your ability to earn is your greatest financial asset. Your real financial value is determined by your ability to earn. Think of yourself as a money-earning machine. Now, consider that all the tasks that you perform offer some value toward this money-earning incapacity. Not every task will offer the greatest value. Some have a high value, while others are low. If you want to become an efficient time manager, then you need to focus on the task that offers the highest value. By doing this, you will contribute not only significantly to your organisation but to yourself and life in general.

Determining the most valuable use of your time is one concept that can apply to every aspect of your life and not just to work. At times, the most valuable usage of your time is to go home after a long and tiring day and get some rest. It might mean eating a healthy meal and exercising. It can also mean spending time with people who lift you up. Sometimes, it can mean simply focusing on proper rest and relaxation. What matters the most is that you are constantly asking yourself this question. This is a great way to eliminate time wasters. If you repeatedly ask yourself this question, you will automatically know the activity you must concentrate on. Once you know the answer, discipline yourself and focus on it until you have achieved it. Whatever it is, complete it before moving on to anything else.

Before you get started, take the time needed to carefully classify the tasks and then ensure that you are on the right track. Any activity that falls in the final quadrant must be eliminated immediately. They are the best doors. Similarly, all that fall into the third quadrant, which includes one that is urgent but isn't important, must be put on hold until the end. Most end up wasting their time performing activities that belong to this quadrant. If a task is not important, but it is urgent but offers little or no value, it's nothing but a waste of your time. Even if it is enjoyable, it doesn't result in anything productive. So, get rid of it. Always start your day by tackling things that fall into the first category and then move on to the second one.

No Procrastination

One thing that usually gets in the way of time management is procrastination. It is not just the thief of time, but of life, too. Were there instances when you put something on hold until the last moment? Even when you knew you had to complete it, you just couldn't. Well, that's what procrastination is about. It is the act of putting things on hold until the last moment. Some believe they work well under pressure, but the truth is that it simply gets in the way of success. It is also a source of severe stress and anxiety. Learning to overcome this and get things done on time can make the difference between success and failure.

We all procrastinate at one point or another. Some do it more frequently than others. Procrastination usually stems from the desire to focus on a short-term reward instead of a long-term gain. For instance, watching an additional episode on Netflix is more appealing than working on a boring presentation. Regardless of how interesting the show is, the presentation will still be due on the same date. By procrastinating, you end up choosing immediate satisfaction instead of growth and progress.

That said, procrastination is not all that bad. We all procrastinate, and this is an undeniable truth. Regardless of how successful an individual is, they would have procrastinated at some point or another. However, there is a difference between how a high producer and a low producer procrastinate. Someone who procrastinates on any activities or tasks that are of barely any value or have no value altogether is known as a high producer. On the other hand, a low producer usually ends up procrastinating on tasks that are of high value and of significant importance. This is the difference between the overall output or results they get. A high producer will still be efficient despite their procrastination, whereas a low producer will not be.

So, to make the most of the time available while maximising your productivity, you need to engage in what is known as creative procrastination. It essentially refers to a process where you need to consciously decide the tasks or items that can be put on hold without harming your productivity. Go through the daily list you were asked to create in one of the previous steps.

Unfortunately, overcoming procrastination is one of those things that is easier said than done. Most of us procrastinate on bigger tasks, especially the most important ones. We do this for a variety of reasons. Whether it's the fear that you will fail, the thought of the task being overwhelming, or anything else along these lines, such things impede success. That said, here are some efficient techniques that can overcome procrastination. Even if you cannot overcome it completely, you can at least manage it so that it doesn't result in time wastage.

Program Your Mind

If you want to overcome procrastination, then it's time to program your mind. Whenever you notice that you're procrastinating, especially when the task is important, repeat a mantra such as, "Do it now!" When you keep repeating such words or phrases, it unconsciously programs your mind to focus on the task that is more important than others. Once you complete this task, you can move on to other things.

Salami Slice Method

The salami slice method is a variation of the technique you introduced in the previous step. If you have a loaf of salami, will you be able to eat it in one bite? Well, the answer is that you obviously cannot. Instead, you need to slice it so that you can eat it. Similarly, you need to salami slice any task on hand. This reduces the size of the task itself and the time involved. Once you have the salami-sliced tasks, work on one small slice at a time. Every time you sit down with a significant task or a challenge, especially something overwhelming, complete it one step at a time. Once you complete the first part, it builds the momentum needed to complete the others.

Sense of Urgency

Our ability to create a sense of urgency is a valuable and rare trait. A tiny fraction of people move quickly to get things done. Most of us are used to procrastinate and putting things on hold or getting distracted in this process. Your ability to set priorities and start and complete the most important task properly will set you apart from your peers. This is also needed for progressing in your career. Focus on developing a reputation by getting started on the most important tasks and completing them quickly and efficiently. Create a sense of urgency for yourself, and you can overcome procrastination.

Single-Minded Focus

If you want to achieve the goals you have established, then you need to stay focused on the task at hand. This is where single handling and concentration step into the picture. Once you are aware of the most important task to be completed, persevere without giving in to any distractions or diversions along the way. You cannot do this unless you can concentrate single-mindedly on the said task. Every other requirement of the job description can be managed via your abilities, intelligence, and creativity. However, you cannot be successful unless you learn to focus on one thing at a time. The first things must be done first and must be done one at a time. Unless you complete the one at hand, do not move on to anything else. If you do not learn to discipline your mind and develop single-minded concentration, you'll end up wasting time, energy, and resources on tasks of low priority and value.

You should always leave sufficient time to deal with tasks of the highest priority. Work out how much time it will take to complete a specific one, and then give yourself a buffer of around 30% for any unexpected interruptions. When you have a decent margin, it becomes easier to deal with any stress that comes along. The two things you need to do to improve your focus are single-handling and avoiding multitasking.

An important technique of time management that anyone can learn is single handling. It essentially refers to the ability to start a task, stay with it, and ensure that it is complete. It means you should not keep picking up or putting down the same one repeatedly or keep shuttling between the two. When you are single handling, you are not supposed to put the task down until it is 100% complete. This requires mental discipline. This technique can apply to any aspect of your life. For instance, if there are multiple emails you need to respond to, then set some time aside for it. During this period, focus only on responding to emails and nothing else. Don't keep shuffling between multiple applications or responding to messages and other forms of communication. Once you start a task, don't move on to anything else unless you have completed it.

Single handling is a great way to improve your overall productivity. Every time you set it down and move on to something else, the momentum and rhythm you have built so far are lost. Because of this, you also lose track of where you last stopped and will need to take the time to restart the next time you go back to the task. This cycle keeps repeating. Had you taken the time needed and completed the first task, you could easily move on to the next one. Instead, you are now dealing with multiple tasks, and none of them is close to completion. Avoid doing this, especially while dealing with tasks of high priority. Ensure that you complete one task and then move on to the next one. This not only improves your overall productivity but ensures efficient time management too.

In the same vein, avoid multitasking. There seem to be plenty of arguments about whether multitasking is beneficial. Some believe their productivity improves significantly when they do this. Others believe working on several things at once only reduces their productivity.

Multitasking refers to the concept of task shifting. As mentioned previously, understand that you cannot do more than one at any given point in time. Even if you try doing another, you need to shift all your focus, attention, and energy to the second. So, when you go back to the previous one, you'll need to shift all of this again to another target. Then you will have to review and bring yourself up to speed on the previous one. When you keep doing this, you are not getting anything done. Instead, the work is piling up while your energy levels are reducing. You are not only wasting time, but exerting more effort than needed for task completion.

The one thing you must focus on is avoiding multitasking and practising single handling. Then there is no time like the present to make this desirable change. Once you do it, you will notice your overall productivity improves. However, without the needed discipline, you cannot make the switch. Hold yourself accountable and ensure that you complete one task at a time.

Time Blocks

To maximise your accomplishments, you need unbroken blocks of time. Suppose the work is important, as the importance of establishing time blocks increases. You will need anywhere between 60-90 minutes to accomplish anything solid and worthwhile. Your mind usually takes up to 30 minutes to fully engage itself in a complicated task. Whether it is planning for an important project, preparing a proposal, or even writing a report, you won't see it through to completion if you don't give yourself time to dive into it. Once you are focused on the task, it takes single-minded concentration, awareness, and creativity for the next 60 minutes or more. This is how focused work is done.

Before you learn to create blocks of time, it's important to ensure that creative tasks aren't mixed with administrative functions. Operational and creative tasks cannot be performed simultaneously. It not only results in multitasking, but it requires a different order of thinking as well. For instance, each of these requires either fast or slow thinking. You cannot do both together. Office or administrative tasks usually require fast and short-term thinking. On the other hand, creative ones require slow thinking because you'll need to thoroughly think things through, plan, and then focus on the application.

Creating blocks of time will improve your overall productivity, efficiency, and effectiveness. Usually, most people are alert and fresh in the morning hours. Try to go to sleep early so that you can wake up early in the morning. As long as you get 6- 7 hours of uninterrupted good quality sleep at night, your body and mind will be energetic and refreshed. This, in turn, makes it easier to focus and get things done quickly. Instead of going to sleep late at night, discipline your body and mind to sleep early and wake up early. Even if you only manage to get 60-90 minutes of uninterrupted work time in the morning, your productivity will be brilliant. This is when your mind is not cluttered by other thoughts and can instead fully focus on the task at hand. Even an hour of uninterrupted productivity is better than 3 hours of hard work. You can also make the most of your lunchtime. It's about relaxing your mind. After working from morning until lunch, take a break. Switch your phone off or put it on silent. Instead of worrying about work or thinking about other things, relax. Once you are relaxed and your body is fed, you can get back to the task at hand. This will give you the peace needed to focus on the most important ones.

Another brilliant strategy that can be used for improving your productivity and single-minded focus while tackling the biggest task is to place a "do not disturb" sign on your door. If you have dedicated space for yourself in the office, this strategy comes in handy. Simply place the sign on the door and ensure that others are aware they are not supposed to disturb you unless it is an emergency. This ensures you will get uninterrupted time to focus on the important matters at hand and minimise distractions as well. Along with this, it teaches others to differentiate between what's important and what's not.

Extra Hours

Another great technique that most executives use is to gain extra hours. We only have 24 hours at our disposal, so how will we gain extra hours? It's simply about planning the day such that you get an extra hour or two to work before everyone else arrives. It means you need to reach your workspace an hour or two before everyone else arrives. This once again gives you uninterrupted time to focus on important tasks. Use that additional hour to organise your workday and try to get as much done as possible with no distractions and interruptions. If you manage to work through lunch, you gain another additional hour of productivity. Similarly, waiting for an hour after everyone leaves also gives you some extra time.

However, ensure that you are not doing this daily. It will result in burnout. This is needed when you believe the task is of utmost importance and you need to complete it quickly. By simply adjusting your day a little, you can gain extra hours and get things done.

Regulate Interruptions

Even if you are working in an extremely focused office environment, you'll still need to deal with interruptions and distractions. On any given day, you will be interrupted quite a few times at work. This is because we live in a world of distractions. Whether it's chat messages, important news, or email threads, different things will take up your time. There are also personal relationships at play, and this makes for the most common workplace distraction. You will still be around many people, and this in itself can distract enough. Unless you can stay completely alone, you will need to learn to manage interruptions and distractions so that it does not get in the way of your productivity.

In this section, let's look at simple suggestions for regulating interruptions and improving your productivity while minimising time wastage.

Deal With Messages and Other Forms of Communication

The most efficient and formal means of communication at any workplace is through email. It is a necessary tool for all types of work. However, it's also the biggest source of distraction in any workplace. Even if it is needed and is the most efficient means to communicate with others, it becomes tedious and distracting. If your phone is constantly pinging notifications about any emails you are receiving or most of your time is spent scrolling through them and replying, you are constantly losing productivity. As important as communication is, understand that excess of it is nothing but an interruption and distraction. Remember, you do not have the time to engage in unnecessary or unimportant communication during a workday. This is a luxury you cannot afford.

Most of us use smartphones. We have come to a situation where the smartphone itself feels like an extension of our body. However, monitoring the time spent on it is important. If most of your productive hours are spent on your phone, you haven't accomplished meaningful productivity by the end of the day. A simple way to regulate distractions is by turning off notifications on unimportant apps. You can give all interested parties your direct contact number in case of an emergency. This also teaches others to prioritise their tasks and determine what is important or not. You should also schedule some time out of your daily routine to check your emails. Ensure that each of these sessions is no longer than 20 minutes. This is sufficient time to check emails, respond to the important ones, and move on. Schedule this time so that you have completed at least one or two of the most important activities before you check your emails. At the end of the day, even if you haven't accomplished all the activities included in your to-do list, you have at least completed the important ones.

Set a Timeline

Before you do anything, you need the plan to deal with any interruptions or problems. The most efficient means to do this is by recognising distractions. Are you wondering how to do this? Well, you need to create a schedule or a timeline, so you'll be aware of all the other things that are potential distractions. Let's assume that you have a list of tasks to be accomplished. Assign a specific period or limit for each of these tasks. This is an effective means to ensure everything is organised. While you are dealing with interruptions, especially when it is one interruption after the other, the chances of procrastinating increase. Instead of completing them as per the established timeline, you'll be left with different things that are yet to be completed at the end of the day if you keep giving in to distractions. While planning, you can adjust the timeframe so that it is in accordance with your realistic working capacity. The timeline also ensures that you are not giving in to any distractions and are instead getting things done. The plan you create will also show the efficient means to deal with any interruptions at work. If someone calls or sends an irrelevant email, you can see that it does not fit within the plan you have drafted. Any activity that is not important or urgent must be eliminated. So, stick to your plan. There's always room to change things later. For now, the idea is just to get things done. If you scroll through any of your social media profiles, the plan you have created will tell you that you shouldn't be doing it. Instead, stay motivated and complete the assigned tasks.

Before you can get started, you will need a plan in place. As mentioned in the previous chapters, you'll need to do this before your actual workday starts. The ideal time to do this is right before you go to bed. This way, when you wake up the following day, you'll have a fairly good idea of all that has to be completed.

Eliminate Self-Imposed Distractions

You need lots of self-control to deal with distractions. In fact, as harsh as it sounds, you are your biggest source of interruptions. After all, regardless of everything that happens, your behaviours and actions are in your control. Even if an interruption or distraction presents itself, how you deal with it matters. If you give in to the urge to keep checking your phone, you need to eliminate it. This cannot be done without self-control. If you don't develop the needed self-control, it can result in self-sabotage. The simplest way to improve your self-control while dealing with distractions is to assign specific breaks for each of the tasks you like to do. Whether it is scrolling through social media, replying to messages, answering calls, or anything else along these lines, give them scheduled breaks. Once you set the time limit for the break, ensure that you do not exceed it. If you give yourself 5 minutes to do this after working for an hour, stick to the 5 minutes limit.

Effective Meetings

If you pull up your weekly schedule, how many meetings are included in it? As a manager, chances are there will be several meetings you need to attend. Not just during the week, but within a day as well. This is an inalienable aspect of your managerial role. After all, you are the communication link between your superiors and others who are a part of your team. Most managers these days are overloaded with multiple meetings, and usually, these meetings are not as productive as they're supposed to be. In fact, attending and conducting meetings is considered a routine and a boring part of any job description. If most of your time is spent attending meetings, it cannot be productive. Also, if the meetings are too long and do not offer any valuable insights or information, they are pointless. You need to understand that it's not just your time that is valuable; you must learn to value others' time as well.

If you want to improve your productivity and overall morale, it is important to understand that a meeting shouldn't be a waste of time. When a meeting has too much of something or it does not focus on the right outcomes, it is pointless. In this section, let's look at some simple ways to ensure that all the meetings you conduct are effective and efficient. In this regard, there are four scenarios you need to consider. The first scenario is where you have too many meetings to deal with. The second scenario is that the meetings take up too much time or are too lengthy. The third scenario is when the meetings aren't as productive as they should be. The last scenario is where the meetings don't have any focus.

You cannot fully focus on the task you have at hand if you are constantly flooded with reminders about the next meeting you need to attend. If you have meetings scheduled every hour or two, it becomes a barrier to your overall productivity. In such instances, you need to learn to say no, especially if the meeting is unhelpful. Understand that not all meetings will be productive. Similarly, if any meeting is unnecessary or there is a more efficient way to do it, do it. All unnecessary meetings must be cancelled. After all, it's not just your time that is important. If the meetings are not productive, the efficient and productive workday is ruined. Avoid doing this. Along with this, ensure that you establish a no-meeting day for yourself every week. On that day, do not schedule any meetings. Instead, focus on only the most important tasks that are associated with your job description.

Another important and commonly occurring scenario is where the meetings go on for too long. If you are wondering whether the duration of the meetings can be shortened, then they probably can. Meetings do not have to be long. People don't have to be sitting around the table hunched over different documents or gadgets for hours together. Such meetings are unproductive. The simplest way to reduce the duration of a meeting is first to understand that time is an incredibly valuable commodity. Every minute saved helps you focus on tasks that are needed for achieving goals. Not just your personal goals, but organisational objectives as well. While you plan the meeting agenda, estimate the time needed to cover each of the topics. Add all of this up and then choose whether the length of the meeting is appropriate. Perhaps you just need 15 minutes, or maybe the meeting will take 45 minutes. Whatever it is, ensure that you are not wasting time available. Don't worry if the meeting is too short. It's perfectly all right. As long as the agenda of the meeting is met, the time doesn't matter. Remember that if the meetings are going on for too long, you will lose your audience's attention. They are also human and will get distracted. Such meetings become unproductive.

Another official means to reduce the length of any meetings is to have stand-up meetings. Standing up for prolonged periods is not comfortable. This, by itself, will shorten a meeting's duration. Will you be comfortable standing for 45 minutes or an hour? In such instances, you will be forced to prioritise the things to be conveyed in the meeting. This reduces the time spent on discussions and improves your productivity.

If you believe the meetings do not have the required focus, then this is something you need to work on. The simplest way through this is by taking the time needed and planning before you even start the meeting. When you plan, you have specific expectations of not just what you want to achieve from the meeting but what others who are taking part in it expect as well. Two simple ways to ensure that your meetings don't lack focus is by identifying the purpose and the goal of the meeting. After this, you will need to share the established agenda with others attending it and offer the required information before the meeting. If you can do this, the meetings will become productive, and they will have better focus. This ensures that important matters are discussed and addressed. Doing this is needed because there are several instances where managers wonder where all their time went when they did not even fulfil the agenda for which the meeting was convened. To ensure this does not happen, you need to plan. Taking a couple of extra minutes to plan is a blessing because it helps save hours later. Also, whenever you are sending the invite to the meeting, ensure that you share the agenda and the context and other relevant information with the attendees. This allows others to prepare and become better participants.

Finally, if you believe the meetings are not as productive as they are supposed to be, then you'll need to change your strategy. The first thing you must focus on is ensuring that the right people are attending the meeting. Regardless of how well-planned the meeting is, if the right participants are missing, it doesn't serve any purpose. For instance, having the marketing team at a meeting that is primarily focused on the sales department doesn't serve any purpose. In such instances, if the right participants are missing, the entire aim of conducting the meeting itself is lost. It's not just about ensuring that the right attendees are a part of the meeting, but also outlining their roles. Similarly, during the meeting, if there are any changes to be made or any specific responsibilities to be allocated, do it. You need to assign action items as you go. If there are different tasks to be completed, create a timeline for them and assign the roles to different people. This gives others a better idea of what they're supposed to be doing and what is expected of them.

PART C: WORK-LIFE BALANCE

CHAPTER 16: REDEFINE WORK-LIFE BALANCE

Chances are, you might have heard the phrase: work-life balance. In regular conversations about stress and wellbeing, self-care routines ate frequently mentioned as an important part of managing stress and promoting overall wellbeing. These routines are often discussed as being essential for maintaining a healthy lifestyle. It is especially needed if you are juggling multiple responsibilities at work, life at home, and other relationships. Without this much-needed work-life balance, you cannot become as productive as you should be.

So, what does work-life balance actually mean? Even if it makes sense intuitively to anyone who reads it, it can be a little elusive when it comes to achieving it. We have all dealt with the feeling of being overwhelmed when the demands are piling up on the work-life scale and start taking over our entire day. You might have also experienced a feeling that you are living life without fulfilling your dreams and desires. This falls on the other side of the scale. Eventually, it increases the feelings of discontentment and slowly results in disengagement. You must learn to manage your time and energy such that it doesn't leave you feeling unsatisfied or discontent. Instead, managing them effectively and efficiently will leave you feeling more satisfied. By learning to strike and maintain a balance, you can avoid mental exhaustion and ensure that you are always your best self.

The term work-life balance is used to describe a situation of a trade-off between the time spent at work and dealing with work-related tasks versus the time focusing on your personal interests and relationships. It also refers to how you will manage professional aspirations of expectations with personal objectives. Everything that is needed for living a well-lived life is included. The concept of trying to reconcile work with life is nothing new. In fact, this concept has been around for centuries. During the early 1900s, reformers were all for fair labour standards at a time when people were used to working more than a hundred hours per week. This is not only exhausting but draining physically, mentally, and emotionally. The term was introduced in the 1980s. Initially, it was a part of the women's liberation movement. It was brought forward to describe the challenges faced by working women, trying to balance their work schedule with family obligations and commitments.

These days, the concept has shifted and includes all genders. It also includes concepts that are not just restricted to families. For instance, it includes stress management, effective time management, and prevention of burnout. Professional culture is changing along with expectations. This results in a clear yet integrated relationship between work and personal time. When you try to establish this concept for yourself, it is seldom straightforward. Managing both these aspects of your life efficiently will improve your overall sense of satisfaction. Previously, it was mentioned that focusing on the different benefits associated with making change automatically includes the motivation needed to do it.

Importance of Work-Life Balance

Your overall health will improve once you learn to manage your work and life. Without this balance, eventually, it will take a toll on your overall sense of wellbeing. For example, if you are working extremely long hours, you will not have the time needed to follow healthy lifestyles such as eating nutritious and regular meals, exercising frequently, and getting sufficient sleep at night. Without doing these things, your health is going to deteriorate. Poor physical health results in poor mental health. This may result in fatigue. Fatigue reduces your overall focus and productivity. The stress you experience, coupled with neglecting healthy habits, increases the risk of substance misuse and other health problems. It also increases the risk of developing unhelpful coping habits. Along with this, it also negatively hampers your relationships. All this will harm the quality of your relationships. Eventually, it will take a toll on your mental and emotional wellbeing. When you cannot function effectively and efficiently, it results in setbacks in your career too.

Work-life balance will result in higher productivity. Working for too long might sound like an idea to improve your productivity. Unfortunately, it doesn't. It reduces your productivity and efficiency. If a machine is overheated, it will sooner or later break down. This is the same thing that happens to your body and mind if you are overworked. It results in mental and physical exhaustion. On the other hand, when you feel supported and engage in a good work-life balance, you will feel better. It leaves you feeling more creative, organised, and connected. A compilation of these factors will make you a better employee.

Another very important gain from being able to balance life and work is your ability to be aware and focus on what you are doing at any given point. This is known as mindfulness. Mindfulness is a difficult state to achieve, especially when you are bothered by a variety of concerns and obligations. If your mind is running at 100 miles an hour, you cannot stay fully focused on anything you are doing. It also results in chaotic thoughts. A combination of these factors automatically increases your stress. It can make you feel overwhelmed. To avoid this, you need a work-life balance.

How to Achieve Work and Life Balance

Talking about it is one thing, but focusing on achieving it is another thing altogether. In this section, you will learn about simple and practical tips that can be easily incorporated to achieve this much-needed balance.

Start Saying No

One of the toughest yet most important soft skills anyone can learn is the art of saying no. It is tricky to put into practice. However, it is needed for establishing and maintaining boundaries. Before you can learn to say no, start by assessing the usual demands of your typical workday.

After this, you need to learn to articulate and then prioritise the different activities and responsibilities you have to fulfil. The simplest technique you can use here is the Eisenhower matrix you were introduced to in the previous parts of this book. By following the Eisenhower matrix, it becomes easier to focus on the tasks that have taken precedence over the others. This, in turn, makes it easier to say no to things that you don't want to do or aren't important to you.

Take Regular Breaks

Taking regular breaks is incredibly important. It helps improve concentration, reduces the stress you experience, makes you feel more engaged, and makes the work enjoyable. This is needed, especially if you work long hours. Even taking a 10–15-minute break after every 75-90 minutes is excellent for improving your productivity. Do this, and your ability to deal with stress improves. This, in turn, reduces the chances of burnout, making it easier to maintain a work-life balance and increase productivity.

Make the Most of Lunchtime

Make the most of your lunch breaks. Even if it is for just 30 minutes, take that time to do something other than work. Don't spend it at your desk and avoid working through lunch. Instead, use it to mindfully enjoy your meal. This also helps reduce any stress you experience. Doing this helps refresh your mind and improve your preparedness to deal with the tasks at hand.

Some Flexibility Is Needed

You cannot balance your life and work unless you have open and honest conversations about what you need or require. Unless you talk to others about these things, you cannot effectively find solutions to the problems. Whether it is more flexible work time or a compressed workweek schedule, talking to others is a good way to reduce any stress you're experiencing. Also, you are the only one that can fully determine what you need or require. Therefore, efficiently communicating these things to others will allow you to find a way to work through them.

Focus on Your Health

To maintain a proper balance, you need to be at your best. To do this, you need to prioritise your physical wellbeing. It's not just about your physical health, but your mental fitness and emotional wellbeing are needed too. Unless you prioritise all this, they will always come second to something or the other. Simple suggestions, such as meditating daily, regular exercise, and spending time with loved ones, will help improve your health in these aspects. Also, investing in your health is one of the best things anyone can do. Unless you prioritise this, no one else can do it for you.

Self-Compassion Helps

If you want to achieve a healthy balance, then you need to let go of all notions of perfectionism. Instead, replace them with self-compassion. Previously, it was mentioned that perfection is nothing but a mirage.

There's no such thing as perfection. You will find flaws in something that looks seemingly perfect at first glance when you look at it too closely or for too long. Instead of chasing perfection, try to do your best. This is constructive, and it focuses on self-compassion. Don't be hard on yourself and cut yourself some slack. It is okay to make mistakes and make wrong decisions too. It's perfectly fine as long as you learn from wrong decisions and do not give up. By indulging in a little self-compassion, it becomes easier to improve your work-life balance.

Communicate Boundaries

A straightforward means to maintain a healthy balance is by establishing strict boundaries between your work and personal life. This means you need to restrict your work to a set of fixed hours per day. Do not exceed it and ensure that you separate these two aspects of your life as much as possible. For instance, if your regular workday ends at 6 pm, then ensure that you leave all work-related worries at work and don't carry them home after this time. Once you are home, it is important to detach from work completely. You don't have to feel guilty for unplugging from work once your workday is over. Doing this reduces any stress you experience.

Invest in Relationships

Humans are social animals, and therefore, relationships play a big role in our life. Not just relationships, but their quality also matters. Investing in meaningful relationships is a way to take care of your mental and emotional wellbeing. When you have people who love and support you, it makes you feel better. Similarly, having a trusted network or group of people as your support system in place gives the motivation and strength needed to get through different challenges. Having a social support network and connections improves your overall sense of wellbeing. Ensure that you surround yourself with people who are positive, optimistic, confident, and share desirable ideals. These traits rub off on you as well.

Schedule Family Time

Unless you prioritise something, you'll never find the time to do it. We all live hectic lives these days. Therefore, you will need to schedule some time to spend with your loved ones as well. Just like you would schedule an office meeting, schedule time to be spent with your family and other loved ones. Once you put it on your calendar, do not make any excuses and stick to it. Show up when you promise, and it will increase the strength of your relationships. You will need to block some time out of your schedule that's entirely devoted to your loved ones.

Prioritise Quality Time

Your time is at your disposal. This means it is only yours and one else's. Therefore, you need to decide how you want to manage it. The best way to go about maintaining a work-life balance is by prioritising quality time. Do not spread yourself thin. If you do this, it will result in a situation where nothing will ever feel truly satisfying. Instead, focus on things that are important to you and add some value to your life. Whether it is learning a new skill, exercising regularly, or anything else, go for it. Learn to clearly identify what you want to do and focus on it. This is how life-enhancing activities can be made a part of your daily life.

Start Small

After going through the different suggestions given here, you might be tempted to do it all at once. However, avoid doing this. If you try to do too many things at once, it will leave you feeling burnt out and more stressed than ever before. Instead, focus on taking it one step at a time. Implement one suggestion and then move on to the next one. This improves overall efficiency while reducing any feeling of being overwhelmed.

Ask for Help

One thing that most high-achieving professionals are guilty of is that they usually take everything upon themselves. They also think that they might end up bothering others if they ask them for help. Thinking, "If I don't do it, who else will? Or, "I'm the one that has to do it all" will build your stress. Instead, ask for help when needed. There is no harm in asking for help. It is a sign of immense self-confidence, esteem, and respect. Knowing when you cannot do something or cannot push yourself beyond a limit is a sign that your boundaries are in place. Unless you ask for it, you cannot get the help that is needed. Doing this gives you a support system that makes it easier to deal with any problems you're facing.

CHAPTER 17: MANAGING YOUR FREE TIME

In the previous part of the book, you were introduced to all things associated with time management. It was repeatedly stated that you need to make the most of the time available. After all, time management is associated with the quality of life you lead and the satisfaction you experience, and it influences all other aspects of living. That said, you also need some free time. It's not just about taking time off work, but learning to make the most of it. When you do this, it finally gives you a much-needed break from everyday stressors and helps you to pursue things you enjoy.

Remember, your body and mind are not a machine that can work tirelessly. It can be quite tempting to keep working with no breaks under the impression that you are being more productive. You cannot rest and recuperate if you don't give yourself a much-needed breather between work. This means you can suffer from the negative effects of being overworked, such as high stress, lack of concentration, and a general sense of being overwhelmed. Taking a break means you can focus on something else and spend your time on how you want to. If you have any interests, passions, or hobbies, now is the time to invest in them. Your free time can also be utilised for revising or brushing up on an old skill or learning any new skills to further your professional career.

How Much Time Do You Have?

The first step in making the most of your time is to determine how much time you have on your hands. You cannot plan things out accordingly unless you know how much time you have. After this, you can start thinking about how it can be spent. This allows you to identify activities that are not only achievable but doable within the time available.

To determine the free time you have, you need to think about your current commitments and any upcoming changes. Take some time for yourself and sit down with a notebook and pen. After this, make a note of all your existing commitments. These commitments will include things at work and at home and in your personal life. Make a note of everything. After this, make a note of things that you know will be changing. For instance, if you have children at home, depending on their school schedule, you'll have more or less time at home. Similarly, making a note of upcoming holidays is helpful when it comes to making the most of the time available.

Clear Intentions Are Needed

The second aspect is to ensure that your intentions are clear when it comes to how you want to spend your free time. You might already know or have an idea of what you usually like to do. For example, you might enjoy playing a sport, reading, or even spending time with your friends. Similarly, there will be instances when you do not know what you want to do. It doesn't matter because you can always use the time available for testing and exploring different things. These two steps can be followed to set clear intentions and then identify the activities you want to do. After this, you simply need to prioritise. You might have a list of hobbies or activities that you want to do. Unfortunately, whenever you get some free time, you might end up doing something else altogether. You might want to focus on activities that are challenging so that you have improved yourself. Similarly, you will also want to do activities you enjoy. Think of activities that you want to do just for the sake of it or feel better. While doing it, whatever it is, make a note.

There will be different activities you will want to focus on. Now, it's time to prioritise. After all, you cannot do everything at once. Instead, start with one thing and then move on to another. For instance, having as much fun as possible might be a priority for the free time you get. This means that most of your free time must be spent doing activities you love and enjoy. Or perhaps you want to prioritise productivity and learning. In that case, you will need to learn something new when you get some time.

Be a Little Flexible

After going through the first two steps, chances are you think that without planning, you cannot make the most of the time available. That said, you need to be a little flexible when it comes to relaxing. Your free time doesn't necessarily have to be as structured as your time spent at work. Instead, it's about flexibility. Life always throws curveballs. For example, you might have different ideas about how you want to spend a weekend. Unfortunately, an important project comes up at work that requires you to work longer hours. In such an instance, feeling disappointed is normal. But, instead of focusing on the disappointment, think about completing the task at hand so that you can move on to something else. By learning to stay a little flexible, you can manage your expectations.

CHAPTER 18: DEAL WITH CHANGES

Even though change is a small word, it can strike fear into the hearts of the mighty. Life is full of change, regardless of whether it is your personal or professional life. Even when it feels like you are living with a personal cloud in your head, it is not permanent. Similarly, even the good times are not permanent. Everything changes, and therefore, learning to manage is needed. If you don't, you will be left behind. Without change, you have stagnation. If you want to grow and make the most of yourself, discover your potential, and maximise the time available, change is needed. Here are some simple suggestions you can use to ensure you are calm and in control, regardless of what you are facing.

The first thing you need to do is ensure that you avoid resisting. In fact, the more you resist it, the more overwhelming it becomes. Refusal is usually an automatic response to change. This response is not only unproductive but gets in the way of getting things done. Remember, you will need to accept it because it is inevitable. The sooner and quicker you do it, the smoother the transition will be.

Regardless of whether it is a change in your personal or professional life, there will be some positive aspects associated with it. Once you focus on the benefits and the positive aspects, embracing change becomes easy. Even a stressful one can breed positive results. Instead of wasting your time thinking about all the things that you don't like, or the challenges associated with them, focus on the benefits it offers. Every change brings with it a set of new opportunities. By focusing on the good, dealing with change becomes manageable. This is a good mindset when it comes to anything in life.

A common reason most fear change is that it brings with it a sense of uncertainty. It refers to things that are beyond your control. When you can focus on the things that you can control, you will feel better. Similarly, make a list of everything you can manage and everything you can do in your power to deal with it. This increases your preparedness, and the change itself becomes less intimidating.

Dealing with a change is easier once you learn to familiarise yourself with it. Do it quickly and jump headfirst into it. It probably seems a little scary, but unless you take the first step, you will never know. Whether it is at the workplace, such as a new system of doing things or a new team, accept it and discover if it works. Go up front and learn about the new thing that is being introduced. The more quickly you get acclimatised to these things, the more familiar they become. Once you are familiar with it, any fear associated with it automatically goes away.

Learning to accept and manage change is perfectly possible. However, if you are focusing on too many things at once, it will become overwhelming. Even if you are extremely adaptable and flexible, trying to alter many things simultaneously will leave you feeling stressed and exhausted. Therefore, it's important that you only deal with one thing at a time. Manage the dynamic world in one area first, and once you are okay with it, move on to the next.

Change seldom affects just one person. Usually, it affects multiple people. It becomes easier to deal with when you have others around you who are sailing in the same boat. When the experience is shared, it creates a unifying experience. However, the group you choose to be a part of also matters. The unifying experience can quickly take on a negative spin if you are not careful. Consider the group you want to be a part of, and then speak to them about the change to sail through it smoothly.

When things change, you need time to get acclimatised to it. Usually, accepting it is not instantaneous. So, understand and accept that it will take time to master. Whether it is a newly updated system of organisation or a different project, it takes time. In the meantime, the only way to not feel discouraged is by exercising patience with yourself. We all desire instant results. That said, without patience, you won't get through it. Don't pile up on the stress you are already experiencing. Instead, cut yourself some slack.

Along with this, focus on asking some productive questions. Doing this will give you the needed insight to make a positive difference. Also, don't put yourself down because you don't understand everything straight away. Every alteration brings with it an opportunity to learn. When asking questions, ask not only the "whys" - ask detailed questions. Asking questions will also make you more accepting of the change.

Most shy away from change because it makes them feel out of control. Instead, take charge of the situation, and you will feel better. Once you start focusing on all things you can control, your ability to deal with the change improves. It will make you feel empowered and give you the strength to face changing circumstances.

Finally, you shouldn't become too comfortable with any change. Familiarise yourself and get adjusted to it. However, if you become too comfortable, it will be fruitless because things will probably alter again. Keep yourself flexible while adjusting.

You can manage change with confidence and peace and become equipped to deal with any that may come along.

Just Enjoy!

Along with the three suggestions mentioned, you need to learn to relax and enjoy your time. This is how you can make the most of the time available. After all, the idea of free time is to recharge your batteries and reduce any stress you are experiencing. Don't try packing your schedule full of things you want to do. You can take it one thing at a time. You don't have to do everything at once. Simply relax and try to make the most of the time available. Even if it is just a night out with people you love, go ahead and indulge. Be mindful of how you spend the time available and make room for things that make you feel good.

Manage You!

CHAPTER 19: LEARNING TO SAY NO

Have you ever been stuck in a situation that could have been avoided if you had just said no? Perhaps you have been stuck working on a weekend when you didn't want to. Or maybe you have done someone else's work that you had no interest in. Whatever the reason, the inability to say no can cause you a lot of stress. Sometimes most say yes, not just because they don't know how to say no, but are hesitant about how the other person will receive the reply. It's hard to say no without focusing on the feelings of the other person.

The one thing you need to understand is that you cannot control how others feel. Regardless of how much you do for others or how selfless you are, you cannot always please others. If you live your life focused on making others feel good, it will ultimately leave you feeling bad. You aren't responsible for what or how others think and feel. All you can do is focus on yourself. If you are struggling to say no because you want to feel accepted at all times, you are focusing on the wrong reasons.

At times, you might say no, but the way you say it renders it ineffective. For instance, if someone asks you to do something and you don't want to, then saying something like, "I would like to help, but I am busy," is vague and ineffective. Not saying it firmly and being vague opens up room for the other person to continue questioning and probing. Instead of giving them such openings, you need to focus on saying no affirmatively. Being affirmative isn't rude or disrespectful. It is about respecting and implementing your boundaries. The inability to say no will make you feel stuck and suffocated. It results in added stress and worries. To ensure this doesn't happen to you, use the different tips given here to learn how to say no effectively.

Just Say It

When it comes to saying no, just go ahead and say it. You don't have to make any excuses or offer lengthy explanations. You don't need to give a reason, and doing so only gives the other person an opening to ask more questions. It also gives them wiggle room to convince you. Instead, just say it. Avoid delaying it and stalling. If you feel you need to, offer a brief explanation, but nothing more. There is no need for it. You needn't feel compelled to go any further into it than needed. The less is better while saying no.

It can be as simple as saying, "No, I cannot do that, but thank you for thinking of me." Try to limit the wording so they can't persuade you. For example, if you say, "No, I don't have time for that task," the person might try to help you organise your responsibilities so that you have more time. By saying no concisely, you save yourself and the other person time and hassle.

Be Assertive

Always be assertive while saying no. You might feel like apologising for saying no or feel you owe them an explanation. Well, you don't. The idea is to be polite and reverse the power dynamics—making it easier to say no. When you say no assertively, it shows you are taking charge of the situation and telling them what you can and cannot do.

Set Your Boundaries

Take the time needed to re-analyse your relationships and then evaluate the role you play in them. This gives you a better sense of your boundaries. Boundaries help you understand your values and acknowledge the things that aren't acceptable. This reduces any internal discord you experience. Also, without boundaries, you can never prioritise yourself. You will be stuck doing things you don't want to do. To avoid such situations, you need to set and implement boundaries.

At times, people resort to manipulative tactics to get their way. So, you need to be aware of them. Avoid stepping into such traps. The simplest way to do this is by realising your boundaries. If something feels amiss, then chances are it is amiss. If something leaves you feeling unsettled or feels like your values are being compromised, then don't do it. Implement your boundaries and stand by them firmly.

Be Firm

While saying no, ensure that you are firm. If not, there is no point in it. Also, it talks more about the other person than you when they cannot accept or respect your refusal. Saying no expresses your boundaries. Don't feel compelled to say yes just to please others. It is perfectly okay to be firm and not give in.

Question Them

Putting the question back to the person asking you is an efficient solution in most work-related situations. Let's assume that your superior asks you to take on multiple tasks at once, and you cannot handle them. In such situations, instead of struggling to say no, simply state what you can or cannot do. You can say something like, "For now, I am working on this, this, and this. So, I am happy to do all that you asked for, but I will need longer for these new tasks. Also, how do you want me to prioritise these tasks?" Instead of saying yes and getting stuck, by effectively questioning the other person, you can get out of the situation. Also, this makes the situation easier to deal with.

It Is Okay to Be Selfish

Whether it is societal conditioning or worries about how others will think and feel, forget about it all. Instead, put yourself first and prioritise your needs. If you have ever travelled in an aeroplane, then you will be aware of the safety instructions. In case of an emergency, passengers must put on their oxygen masks first before helping others. Regardless of how good your intentions are, you cannot be much help to anyone if you cannot help yourself. This is the reason you need to prioritise yourself. Understand that prioritising yourself is not the same as being selfish. If you prioritise everyone else's needs over your own, then your overall productivity will suffer. The difference between those who are successful and those who are not is that the former is good at saying no.

CHAPTER 20: FOCUS ON SELF-CARE

An excellent manager, or any leader for that matter, is focused on taking care of their team. This is a big responsibility to fulfil along with any business goals or targets they have. This level of care that they need to take can make it seem as if it's all about being selfless. However, this is not how life works. A successful leader and manager is someone who understands it's not just about taking care of others, but themselves, too. If you don't take the time needed for self-care, you will inevitably run ragged.

So, what does self-care mean? It probably brings to mind a day spent at the spa or a morning run. This is not entirely wrong, but there is so much more to the concept of self-care than just this. It's essentially about doing right by yourself. It's about standing up for your wellbeing and having your own back before helping anyone else. So, it includes a variety of things. Self-care refers to different activities and practices that you deliberately choose and engage in regularly to maintain and improve your overall sense of wellbeing, including health. Remember, the activity you choose for self-care must be a deliberate choice, and it must be indulged in regularly. It is not a random occurrence or a one-off thing. It needs to be a part of your daily life. Unless you get into the habit of engaging in self-care regularly, you cannot improve your overall sense of wellbeing.

Here is a simple example of how self-care is needed. A professional athlete should not only focus on training regularly and consistently, but should focus on recovery, too. This is needed for their performance. They are not only serious about the hard work associated with training but recovery after it, too. This is the same logic you need to use as a manager. It's not humanly possible for anyone to stay in their performance mode 24/7. Over time, effectiveness diminishes. However, if you invest in a little recovery and start taking care of yourself, you'll be more effective at your job. It's not just needed for maintaining your physical, emotional, and mental wellbeing, but it is needed for becoming a better manager as well. When you are running low on energy and your motivation and mood are all over the place, you cannot be a strong and compassionate leader.

When you follow a consistent self-care routine, it helps regulate your energy levels, builds resilience, and makes you more mindful. It is also needed for becoming happier and more compassionate, maintaining an optimistic mindset, and becoming consistent in your leadership. And you can get more done, improve your efficiency and productivity, and set a higher standard for others. A mix of all these factors mentioned until now will automatically ensure that you are setting a good example for others to follow. All the benefits associated with self-care cannot be overlooked.

If you are interested in making self-care a part of your life, here are some simple suggestions that can be followed.

Physical Self-Care

An important aspect of self-care is to understand the intricate relationship between your body and mind. You might have heard that sleep is important. Have you ever wondered why? Take a moment to think about it, and the answer will come to you. Will you feel energetic if you want to go to bed late at night and have to wake up early in the morning? Chances are that you will not feel energetic. You'll feel sleepy most of the day. In such an instance, can you be productive? On the other hand, have you ever noticed that not only your energy but motivation levels, as well as the spirit to get things done, are higher when you get sufficient rest? This is why sleep is important. Along the same lines, you need to focus on different aspects of your physical health to improve your overall sense of wellbeing.

Physical self-care involves getting sufficient rest, exercising regularly, and consuming healthy and well-balanced meals. These are the three pillars upon which your physical wellbeing rests. Even if one of them is compromised, your overall health will suffer in one form or another. Unless you have sufficient rest, your body cannot work effectively and efficiently. Following a realistic and consistent sleep schedule and making time for quick breaks throughout your workday will improve your productivity. It also reduces the chances of burnout. Similarly, when you exercise regularly, it helps refresh your body physically. It also increases the production of feel-good hormones and makes it easier to fall asleep at night. Along with that, eating healthy and nutritious food provides your body with the nutrition it requires. When you give your body the right fuel, its ability to function efficiently improves.

Emotional Self-Care

Any leadership role, such as that of the manager, takes a toll on your emotional wellbeing. Some common responsibilities you shoulder include ensuring that your team is led toward a common goal, supporting their interests, and being emotionally present to recognise that they are facing challenges or struggles. You'll need to do all this while you are managing your responsibilities and pressures and stress. Doing all this is not easy, and it takes a toll on your emotional health. Given the fact that you are in a leadership position, you might feel that you cannot show any emotional struggles you are facing. Leadership can make it feel as if you are expected to live up to incredibly high standards for the sake of others who are counting on you. Most managers believe they need always to be okay even when they don't feel like it because others are counting on them.

Instead of believing this popular opinion, it's better to be in touch with your emotional self. Being in touch with your emotions doesn't mean you let them overwhelm or regulate you. It's about emotional intelligence when it comes to handling yourself. You can be open about your emotions without letting them govern you. Sharing your vulnerabilities doesn't make you weak, and you can set a good example by showing your team what self-care looks like.

The simplest way to take care of your emotional wellbeing is by managing your stress levels. Be honest about the stress you are experiencing because no one else can shoulder it for you. Similarly, be honest about your workload and all that you can and cannot do. It's okay to try to do your best, but pushing yourself past your breaking point is seldom desirable.

Focus on setting realistic targets that do not overwhelm you with stress.

How you talk about yourself plays a massive role in how you feel about yourself. If your internal dialogue is riddled with negativity and pessimism, you cannot feel good about yourself or anything that you are doing. By reflecting compassionately on yourself, you can improve your self-talk. This, in turn, gives you the motivational fuel needed to keep going. There is no point in putting yourself down, and it never leads to anything good.

A powerful form of self-care is caring for others. A random act of kindness can leave anyone feeling good. Whether it is buying your team members a cup of coffee or taking them out for a meal, or even helping a junior with their work, do it if you can be effective, regardless of how big or small it is.

Mental Self-Care

Dealing with different responsibilities, fulfilling various obligations, and handling multiple roles requires lots of mental bandwidth. As a manager, you need to do all the above and much more. You also need to focus on your team's growth and development, achieve established goals, deal with deadlines, and so on. While doing all this, forgetting about yourself is quite easy. Unless you get sufficient "me time," you cannot function as intended. Mental self-care is so much more than simply stepping away from your desk. It is about giving your brain a break and your mind some peace. You need to schedule some time out of your daily routine to focus on activities that leave you feeling good about yourself. Whatever it is, focus on doing things you genuinely enjoy. The thought of taking some time out of a fully packed schedule can make it feel as if downtime is nothing but a dream. You can do this, provided you are interested in making a few changes.

Take time to decompress. This is a vital part of any self-care routine. Take the time needed to check in with yourself. Think of it as a daily review meeting with yourself. Find out what is bothering you and the source of any stress you are experiencing. When you feel overwhelmed, take a break from the task at hand and slow down. When you slow down, your problem-solving abilities improve. It also gives you a chance to think more creatively.

You need to do things that make you happy. If you have any hobbies or interests, spend some time on them. You don't have to spend hours every day. Even as little as 30 minutes dedicated to activities you love and enjoy do the trick; remember, it is about the little things in life. Don't get so busy with work that you forget about living.

If you don't have any hobbies but want to pick up a new hobby or learn a skill, do it. Learning something re-energises your mind and helps you focus on value-added tasks. If you want to learn to play an instrument or want to learn a new language, what is stopping you? Unless you make time in your schedule for this, focusing on your interests will never be a priority.

Social Self-Care

Social wellbeing is included in self-care. Our lives aren't restricted to work, and they include relationships beyond those with colleagues and peers.

The first thing you need to do is establish some boundaries and stick to them. If you are usually in the habit of cancelling social commitments due to work or any other work-related reason, stop doing it. This isn't good. Even if it feels like a situation is impossible to get away from, you still have a choice. It is perfectly okay to prioritise work when needed. However, if work becomes your only priority, the quality of your life will suffer. Also, you needn't feel guilty about this. Having a positive and satisfying social life is good for your mental and emotional wellbeing too.

When things get challenging, do you have people to turn to? If you do, then value these relationships. You need a support system in place that will get you through tough times. You also need others to share your happiness and success with, too. Without these people, life becomes lonely. If you are feeling overwhelmed or burned out, then it is time to reach out to your support system.

You must schedule some time for your loved ones and family. Without this, you cannot build and maintain healthy and meaningful relationships. Without these relationships, your overall sense of wellbeing will suffer. Even if you need to write it down in your schedule, go ahead and do it. Value the time spent with your loved ones. It is as important as a business meeting, often more important. When you prioritise spending time with people who make you feel better, it is good for your mental and emotional health.

Personal Self-Care

Life is so much more than just doing your work and moving ahead in your career. It's also about connecting with your inner self and finding a deeper meaning in life. Therefore, personal self-care must also be a part of your self-care routine. A basic thing you can do is to learn to spend some time by yourself. Spending time mindfully with no distractions is a great way to tune into your inner self. It helps get over the distractions of daily life and find peace within. When your head is not overrun by thoughts, worries, and other responsibilities, you can finally focus on who you are as an individual.

Focus on connecting with yourself as well as nature. Spending time outdoors and reconnecting with nature is a healing experience by itself.

Whether it is walking barefoot on the grass or spending time at the beach, go ahead and do it. Get out of your work cubicle and head outdoors. Take a moment to smell the roses and breathe some fresh air. This helps rejuvenate your body and mind.

Finally, find someone or something that inspires you. Whatever it is, spend time doing things that light you up from the inside. Anything can be a source of inspiration. Whether it is engaging in a hobby or spending time with people who inspire you, make time for it. Once you prioritise, you will realise there is an endless supply of inspiration. This is needed to keep going, especially when the going gets tough.

CHAPTER 21: MEANINGFUL RELATIONSHIPS

Humans are social animals, and therefore, relationships are of great importance. Regardless of whether it's a personal or professional relationship, we are all interacting with others daily. Building better relationships at the workplace will make your career more meaningful. When you have a large and diverse network of connections with different people, it becomes an invaluable resource. Whether it is a little support that is needed or advice, this network comes in handy. In this section, we will look at some simple suggestions that can build meaningful relationships at work.

Do the Grunt Work

The first thing you need to do is prepare yourself for a little effort. You cannot build a successful relationship without putting in the work. It doesn't mean you need to put in the effort with everyone you come across. However, ensure that you do this, especially with people you work with or come into contact with regularly and frequently. It not only makes things more comfortable, but is conducive to productivity as well. For instance, if you have a good relationship with all your team members, your ability to motivate, encourage, and mentor them improves. This creates a highly productive team. It also allows you to get to know your team better.

Avoid Distractions

We are all surrounded by different types of distractions - whether it's an electronic device or our thoughts, distractions are everywhere. Tuning out these diversions is not always easy. However, doing it is needed. This is especially true when it comes to relationships. When someone is talking to you or trying to get in touch with you, ensure that you give them your full and undivided attention. This means getting rid of all distractions and simply concentrating on what they are saying.

Help Others

Another great way to build meaningful relationships at work is by being of assistance to others. Others might require help, but they don't know how to ask for it or approach the person. In such instances, simply ask them how you can make their job easier or talk about the help you can provide. This is not only a simple thing to do, but is a critical habit for most managers. However, when you are doing this, ensure that you do not take on more than you can handle. Just because you want to help others doesn't mean you should make your life more complicated than it needs to be. Offer assistance only to the degree that is comfortable for you.

Trust Is Vital

If you tell someone something, ensure that you stand by it. If you make a promise, you must fulfil it. This is the only way to build trust. It also shows that others can count on you and that you are dependable. Whatever the promise, always keep your word. This is the foundation for an excellent working relationship. If you offer to help someone learn a new process, ensure that you do it. Don't make promises without being able to follow through. This is helpful advice that comes in handy in your relationships as well.

It's Not You

One thing you must not do is take things personally at work. Even if your superior criticises you or you receive some negative feedback, take it constructively. Don't take it personally and don't let it ruin your day. Remember, you have a team to look after. Instead of getting defensive and emotional when you receive feedback, approach it from a logical and professional perspective. This makes it easier to find areas where there is scope for improvement. Also, when you take things personally, it will impede your productivity. Don't let someone else's bad mood ruin your day because your productivity will suffer.

Love Thy Neighbour

Treat others how you want to be treated. This is basic psychology that comes in handy in all relationships. If you want others to respect you, then you need to be respectful. Similarly, if you want them to be kind, you will need to show kindness. Take the first step and do what you want others to do. Along the same lines, ensure that you show respect. This is the golden rule for building meaningful relationships at work. Whether it is your co-workers, subordinates, or even superiors, always be respectful. It can be something as simple as listening to what others are saying without interrupting. Even if they say things you do not agree with, keep your opinions to yourself until you are asked for them. Even a contradicting opinion can be stated peacefully and constructively.

No "I" in Team

You are a manager, and therefore you need to be a team player. You're not just a link between corporate and employees, but you are also a link between all the members of your team. So, remember that there is no "I" in the word team. This age-proverb is extremely useful for building relationships. When you become a team player, it creates a vibrant culture that thrives on productivity.

We all like to be praised and crave appreciation. If someone does something well, express your gratitude and appreciation. Don't shy away from doing this. Others should also know that they are doing a good job. This gives them the internal motivation needed to keep going. It's always the little things that make a big difference.

While dealing with any challenges at work, be honest about them. You don't have to put on a brave face; if you need help, ask for it. Showing honesty and a little vulnerability goes a long way in establishing meaningful relationships at work.

CHAPTER 22: PREVENTING BURNOUT

Burnout is a state of physical, emotional, and mental exhaustion that is caused by prolonged or excessive stress. It can cause a variety of symptoms, including fatigue, irritability, insomnia, and an overall decrease in productivity. This is a serious condition that can have harmful effects on your health and wellbeing if left unchecked. However, there are things you can do to prevent or manage it.

If you're experiencing any of the warning signs of burnout, it's vital to address the problem before it gets worse. This chapter will explore the warning signs and causes of burnout in more detail, as well as provide some tips on how to prevent or manage it. By the end of this chapter, you should have a better understanding of how to protect yourself and improve your self-management skills.

Warning Signs

At some point in our lives, we've all felt the effects of burnout. Whether it's from a demanding job, caring for our families, or simply trying to keep up with the demands of day-to-day life, we've all been there. And while it may seem like there's no way out, there are quite a few things you can do to help yourself. First, it's important to recognise the signs. These can include feeling overwhelmed, exhausted, or unable to focus.

If you're experiencing any of these symptoms, it's crucial to take a step back and reassess your priorities. Sometimes, all it takes is a little self-care - whether that means taking a break from work, spending time with loved ones, or simply getting some extra sleep. But if you find that you're struggling to cope, it might be time to seek professional help.

There are many resources available to those who are struggling with burnout, and seeking help is a sign of strength, not weakness. So, if you're feeling overwhelmed, reach out for help. You deserve it. Here are some of the warning signs:

Feeling Exhausted All the Time

Feeling exhausted all the time is one of the most common warning signs. If you find that you're constantly tired, even after getting a good night's sleep, it's a sign that your body is under immense stress. Feeling exhausted can also be accompanied by other symptoms, such as difficulty concentrating, irritability, and headaches. If you're experiencing any of these symptoms, it's critical to take a step back and assess how you're feeling.

Are you constantly running on empty? Are you putting your own needs last? If so, it's time to make some changes. Taking some time for yourself, even if it's just a few minutes each day, can make a big difference. If you're still struggling to manage your stress, consider speaking to a therapist or counsellor. They can help you develop healthy coping mechanisms and get to the root of your stressors.

Increased Cynicism or Negative Outlook

In the early stages, you might become increasingly cynical. You start to see the world through a lens of negativity, and it's hard to find anything that brings you joy. This is because burnout causes you to feel you're carrying the weight of the world on your shoulders.

All the little day-to-day stresses can feel like too much, and it's easy to get overwhelmed. If you find yourself feeling this way, take some time for yourself. Make sure to schedule some downtime and try to do things you enjoy. This way, you can recharge your batteries and get back to a more positive outlook on life.

Losing Interest in Work

It's normal to have times when you don't feel motivated at work. Maybe you're stuck in a rut or feeling uninspired by your current project. However, if you find that you're consistently struggling to care about your work, it could be a sign of burnout. When you're experiencing it, even simple tasks can feel overwhelming and impossible to complete.

You might lose interest in things that you used to enjoy and feel you're just going through the motions. If you're concerned that you might be burnt out, reach out for help. Talk to your supervisor, or see a therapist who can help you manage your stress. Taking action early can help prevent this from becoming a more serious problem.

Feeling Like You're Not Accomplishing Anything

It's easy to feel you're not accomplishing anything when you're burnt out. After all, when you're feeling exhausted and overwhelmed, even the simplest tasks can seem challenging. If you find yourself feeling this way regularly, take steps to address the issue. Otherwise, you might feel like your life is spiralling out of control.

One of the best things you can do is to set small goals for yourself and break them down into manageable steps. This way, you can see your progress and feel a sense of accomplishment as you check each task off your list.

Additionally, don't be afraid to ask for help when you're feeling overwhelmed. Friends and family members can often provide valuable assistance and support. Finally, schedule some time for relaxation and fun activities you enjoy. This will help to restore your sense of balance and give you the energy you need to keep going.

Decreased Productivity

Many of us have experienced the feeling of being burnt out at some point in our lives. Whether it's from work, school, or another area of life, constantly being exhausted can take a toll on our physical and mental health. One warning sign is decreased productivity. If you find that you're struggling to complete tasks you used to do with ease, it may be a sign that you're feeling overwhelmed.

If you're experiencing any of these symptoms, take a step back and reassess your priorities. What can you eliminate from your plate to focus on the most important tasks? Is there someone who can help you with some of your responsibilities? Don't be afraid to delegate or ask for help when you're feeling overwhelmed. Make sure you're taking care of yourself mentally and physically, and reach out for help if you need it.

Avoiding People

If you find that you're avoiding social situations more than usual, it can be a sign that you're experiencing burnout. When we're burnt out, we often want to retreat from the world and spend time alone. This is because being around other people can feel overwhelming and draining. We can feel like we can't keep up with the pace of life or have anything meaningful to say.

If you find yourself feeling this way, take some time for yourself. This might mean saying no to invitations, taking a break from work, or carving out some alone time each day. However, don't isolate yourself completely. Staying connected to others can help provide support when you're struggling. Make sure you're maintaining some social interactions, even if they're on a small scale.

According to the Mayo Clinic, burnout is a state of physical, emotional, and mental exhaustion that is caused by prolonged or chronic stress. Symptoms include feeling overwhelmed, detached, or hopeless, experiencing problems with sleep or concentration, and turning to unhealthy coping mechanisms, such as alcohol or drugs. One warning sign is isolating yourself from others.

When you're overwhelmed by stress, it can be tempting to withdraw from social activities and hole up at home. However, this isolation can worsen feelings of loneliness and despair, making it even harder to cope with stress. If you find yourself retreating from your social life, it can be a sign that you're on the verge of one. Reaching out to a trusted friend or family member can help you feel connected and supported, making it easier to manage stress.

Feeling Anxious, Stressed, or Overwhelmed

If you're feeling anxious, stressed, or overwhelmed, that's a red flag. You might feel like you can't keep going and that everything is just too much. If you're struggling to cope with stress, take steps to prevent it. Recognising the warning signs is the first step.

If you're feeling anxious, stressed, or overwhelmed regularly, take a step back and assess your situation. Are you taking on too much? Do you need to simplify your life? Are you getting enough rest? Taking action can help you avoid its effects and stay healthy, both physically and mentally.

Changes in Eating or Sleeping Habits

Whether it's from working too much, caring for a sick relative, or dealing with an ongoing stressor, burnout can take a toll on your mental and physical health. One of the warning signs is changes in your eating or sleeping habits. If you find yourself skipping meals, overeating, or having difficulty falling asleep, it can be a sign that you're heading critically close to burnout.

Eating and sleeping are essential for good health, and when they're disrupted, it can lead to a cascade of other problems. If you're struggling to keep up with your usual eating and sleeping patterns, assess your overall stress levels. Making time for self-care can help you avoid burnout and stay on top of your game.

Illness

When you're burned out, it's hard to muster up the energy to do even the simplest tasks. If you're normally a healthy person, you might find that you're suddenly getting sick more often. This is because burnout weakens your immune system, making you more susceptible to illness. If you find that you're constantly exhausted and getting sick more often than usual, it's a warning sign that you might be burning out.

If you're struggling, get help. Burnout can have serious consequences if left untreated, so reach out to a doctor or therapist if you're feeling overwhelmed. Many self-care techniques can help reduce stress and promote relaxation. Taking some time for yourself may be the best way to nip it in the bud.

Causes of Burnout

Burnout can result from several factors, including work pressure, family responsibilities, caregiving, and chronic illness. When we're burning out, we can feel overwhelmed, hopeless, and unable to cope. We might also experience physical symptoms such as fatigue, headaches, and gastrointestinal problems. If left untreated, burnout can lead to serious health problems such as anxiety, depression, and heart disease.

Here are some common causes:

Unreasonable Expectations

Often, the cause is simply that we have too many demands on our time and energy. We expect ourselves to be perfect, always to be available, and never to make mistakes. But the reality is that we're human, and we simply can't meet those impossible standards.

So how do we deal with unreasonable expectations? First, we must recognise when things are taking a toll on our wellbeing. If we're regularly finding ourselves feeling stressed out or unable to enjoy our lives, it's time to take a step back and reassess our priorities. From there, we can start setting realistic boundaries and learning to say "no" when needed. It won't be easy, but making these changes can help us avoid exhaustion and live happier, more balanced lives.

Lack of Control

One of the potential causes is a lack of control. When we feel like we're not in control of our lives, it's easy to become overwhelmed and feel like everything is out of our hands. This can lead to a feeling of hopelessness and, eventually, burnout. Trying to do too much can be just as damaging as doing nothing at all.

To avoid this, it's crucial to take back control when we can. That might mean saying no to some things, delegating or asking for help when needed, and making sure we're taking care of ourselves both physically and mentally. So, find a balance, and focus on the things you can control. You'll be much better off for it in the long run.

Poor Work/Life Balance

Now, this is one of the big ones. When you're constantly pulled in different directions, it's tough to find time to relax and recharge. As a result, you're more likely to feel overwhelmed and stressed out.

If you're struggling with burnout, take a step back and assess your work/life balance. Are you putting in too many hours at work? Are you taking on too many responsibilities outside of work? If so, it's vital to make some changes. Create boundaries between work and life, and make sure to schedule time for yourself. It might seem difficult at first, but it's essential.

Lack of Support

It's no secret that burnout is a major problem in the workplace. And while many factors can contribute to it, one of the most common is a lack of support. Whether its insufficient resources, unrealistic deadlines, or simply not having enough help, when employees feel like they're struggling to do their job with no help, then they'll hit rock bottom.

And unfortunately, once someone reaches the point of full-on burnout, it can be very difficult to recover. That's why it's so crucial for employers to provide their employees with the support they need. By ensuring that employees have the resources and assistance they need to do their job, employers can help create a healthy and productive work environment.

Job Insecurity

Job insecurity is one of the leading causes. When you feel like your job is in danger, it's natural to want to work harder to prove your worth. However, this can quickly lead to overwhelming feelings and exhaustion. It's a vicious cycle that can be difficult to break free from.

If you're constantly worrying about whether you're going to keep your job, find ways to manage your stress. This might include exercise, relaxation techniques, or talking to a therapist. Remember, your mental health is just as important as your job. Don't be afraid to take care of yourself.

Unclear Job Role

Another major cause is having an unclear job role. If you're not sure what's expected of you at work or if your job duties are constantly changing, it's difficult to stay motivated. You might feel you're just going through the motions, and that can lead to feelings of hopelessness and detachment. If you're suffering from burnout, talk to your boss or HR department about your concerns, and look for ways to simplify your workload.

Conflicting Values

It's not uncommon for people to feel conflicting emotions about their work. On the one hand, you might feel passionate and committed to your career; on the other hand, you might feel drained and overloaded. When these conflicting emotions are left unresolved, it can lead to exhaustion.

One of the main causes of weariness is conflicting values. For example, someone may appreciate creativity and innovation, yet they may be trapped in a job that demands them to adhere to rigid regulations and processes. Or someone may admire independence but be stuck in a position that requires extensive collaboration with others. These conflicting values can lead to feelings of frustration, resentment, and disillusionment, which can eventually lead to fatigue.

If you're struggling with conflicting values at work, take some time to reflect on what's most important to you. What do you value most in your work? Once you have a clear sense of your values, you can start working on aligning your work with those values. This can mean looking for a new job, or it can mean making some changes in your current job. Either way, taking action to align your work with your values is an important step.

Demanding Work Schedule

While a demanding work schedule can be a factor, it's not the only one. Other potential causes include a lack of control over one's work, insufficient support from co-workers or supervisors, and a lack of clarity about job expectations. In addition, personal stressors can compound job stress, such as financial problems or family issues. The key to preventing burnout is to identify early warning signs and take steps to address them.

When your job requires you to work long hours, it's important to manage your time and energy. This might include scheduling breaks, delegating tasks, and setting boundaries. Make time for yourself outside of work. Pursue hobbies, spend time with loved ones, and take care of your physical health. If you're finding that your work schedule is consistently putting you under excessive stress, it might be time to have a conversation with your supervisor about making some changes. By taking action early, you can prevent burnout before it has a chance to take hold.

High-Pressure Environment

Working in a high-pressure environment is one of the most common reasons for burnout. Unrealistic deadlines, constant demands, and little to no opportunity for rest or relaxation often characterise high-pressure environments. This can lead to feelings of being overwhelmed, anxiety, and even depression.

If you're struggling to cope in a high-pressure environment, take some time for yourself outside of work. Make sure to schedule some leisure time, and try to stick to it. This can be anything from reading a book, going for a walk, or taking a yoga class. It's crucial to find an activity that helps you relax and avoid sluggishness.

Toxic Workplace

Though it might seem like the busyness of work is the primary cause of over-tiredness, studies have shown that it is the workplace itself that is to blame more often than not. This is because when we don't feel supported or appreciated at our job, we are far more likely to experience feelings of stress and anxiety. Additionally, a toxic workplace can also lead to physical health problems such as headaches and insomnia.

If you find yourself feeling constantly drained, both mentally and physically, it might be time to assess your work environment. Do you feel you can openly communicate with your boss? Do you feel like your opinion is valued? If the answer to both is no, then it might be time to look for a new job. Don't let yourself be a victim of a toxic workplace - take control of your life and make a change.

How to Prevent Burnout

Anyone who has ever experienced burnout knows it is not a pleasant feeling. Characterised by feelings of exhaustion, cynicism, and low motivation, burnout can make it difficult to function both professionally and personally. It is critical to prevent this for several reasons. First, it can lead to a decline in work performance. Second, it can negatively affect your health. And third, it can damage your relationships.

The good news is that there are several things you can do to prevent this from happening. Taking regular breaks, setting realistic goals, and maintaining a healthy lifestyle are all key to keeping your energy levels up. So, if you're feeling burnt out, take some time for yourself and make some changes to prevent further damage. Here are some tips on how to prevent burnout:

Set Realistic Expectations

One of the most important things you can do is to set realistic expectations. If you are constantly putting pressure on yourself to meet unrealistic goals, it is only a matter of time before you start to feel overwhelmed and exhausted. Instead, take a step back and assess what you can realistically accomplish in the short and long term.

Once you have a clearer picture of what you can realistically achieve, you can start setting goals that are achievable and maintainable. Additionally, try to schedule regular breaks throughout your day so that you can take some time for yourself. Even if it is just a few minutes, taking some time to relax and rejuvenate will help.

Find a Balance between Work and Life

It's no secret that today's work culture can be pretty intense. With constant deadlines and the pressure to always be "on," it's easy to get overwhelmed. If you're not careful, all of that stress can lead to something worse. So how can you prevent burnout before it happens? The key is to find a balance between work and life. Take some time for yourself every day, even if it's just a few minutes.

Step away from your work, clear your mind, and do something that you enjoy. It might seem like a small thing, but it can make a big difference in your overall wellbeing. You should also try to keep a healthy perspective on your work. Remember that it's just one part of your life, and don't let it consume you. If you can find a balance between work and life, you'll be much less likely to experience fatigue.

Seek Support from Others

It's easy to get caught up in the hustle and bustle of everyday life and push yourself too hard. Over time, this can lead to burnout. If you're feeling overwhelmed and exhausted, it's crucial to seek support from others. Talking to a trusted friend or family member can help you feel more connected and less alone.

Joining a support group can also be beneficial. This allows you to share your experiences with others who understand what you're going through. Additionally, working with a therapist can provide you with valuable tools for managing stress and coping with difficult emotions. If you're struggling, reach out for help. It makes a world of difference.

Take Control of Your Job

Work can be a fulfilling and rewarding experience. It can also be a major source of stress and anxiety. When work feels like a burden, it's vital to take action to prevent exhaustion. One of the best ways to do this is to take control of your job. Set realistic goals, delegate tasks when possible, and take regular breaks. It's also crucial to focus on the positive aspects of your job and to build a supportive network of colleagues and friends. By taking these steps, you can prevent tiredness and create a more positive work-life balance.

Take Time for Yourself

We live in a world that is always on. With 24/7 access to email, social media, and work, it's easy to burn out. That's why it's critical to take time for yourself. Set aside some time each day to do something that you enjoy with no stress or obligations. It could be something as simple as reading a book, taking a walk, or listening to music.

Whatever it is, make sure it's something that you truly enjoy and helps you relax. You might also want to consider scheduling some "me time" into your week. This could be a massage, a manicure/pedicure, or a night out with friends. Taking some time for yourself will help you prevent weariness and feel refreshed and ready to take on the world.

Don't Be Afraid to Say No

We all have too much on our plates. Whether it's work, family, or social obligations, it's tough to find the time to relax and recharge. And when we're constantly running on empty, it's only a matter of time before we start to feel burnt out. If you're feeling overwhelmed, don't be afraid to say no. It's okay to turn down that extra project at work or cancel plans with friends.

Set Boundaries

It's crucial to set boundaries in life to prevent feeling burnt out. When we don't set boundaries, we can quickly become overwhelmed by everything that's on our plate. We might feel like we have to do everything and be everything to everyone, and that can lead to feelings of intense stress and anxiety.

It's vital to learn how to say no, and to set limits on what you're willing to do. That doesn't mean you're a bad person - it just means that you're taking care of yourself. Make time for things that you enjoy and refuel your batteries regularly. When you take care of yourself, you're better able to take care of others. Your mind and body will thank you for it.

Find a Way to Enjoy Your Work

We've all been there before. You're working on a project that you're passionate about, but after a few days (or weeks or months), you start to feel burnt out. The passion that you once felt is gone, and all that's left is a sense of dread and indifference. So how can you prevent burnout before it happens? The key is to find a way to enjoy your work, even when the going gets tough.

For some people, this means taking regular breaks to recharge their batteries. Others find that listening to music or podcasts while they work helps to keep them focused and motivated. The important thing is to find a way to stay engaged with your work, even when the going gets tough.

Talk to Your Boss about Your Concerns

No one wants to get to the point of burnout at work. That's why it's necessary to nip the problem in the bud by talking to your boss about your concerns before things get too out of hand. Your boss might not be aware of how much you're doing or how stressed you're feeling, so it's crucial to voice your concerns early on.

Come up with a plan together on how you can lighten your workload and make your job more manageable. This might involve delegating some of your tasks to other team members or taking on a less demanding role for a while. Whatever the solution, talking to your boss is the first step to taking control of the situation.

Burnout is a serious problem that can hurt your health and wellbeing. This chapter has discussed some warning signs to watch out for and given some tips on how to prevent them. From exhaustion and cynicism to a loss of motivation and a sense of dread, it can creep up on you when you least expect it.

If you're starting to feel burnt out, take action immediately. Talk to your boss about your concerns and try to lighten your workload. Make time for things that you enjoy, and learn how to set boundaries. And most importantly, take care of yourself. By taking these steps, you can prevent burnout and live a happier, healthier life.

CONCLUSION

There's a Chinese proverb that says if you want one year of prosperity, grow grain. If you want ten years, grow a tree. If you want a hundred years, grow men.

Now, this can apply to every facet of life, whether it's business, politics, or anything else. However, we often forget that it can apply to us. If you, as an individual, want success, whether in everyday life, relationships, work or family, then you need to grow. You need to work on yourself and develop in such a way that you really are living your full potential.

There's no benefit from staying stagnant. More of the same is rarely better, and the sooner you realise that change can be liberating, the faster your growth will come. Besides, as a manager, you should lead by example. And what better way to do this than to show you can apply these skills to your own life?

Hopefully, this book has given you the tools and put you on the track to truly making a difference in your life as a manager and as a person. But remember, it has to start with you. Take that leap, believe in what these skills can do for you, and watch your life become that much richer.

REFERENCES

7 Essential Self-Management Skills: Definition, Examples, and Tips. (2021, March 5). Ali Abdaal. https://aliabdaal.com/self-management-skills/#-organisation

7 Ways to Practice Conscientiousness at Work. (n.d.). Indeed, Career Guide. https://www.indeed.com/career-advice/career-development/how-to-be-conscientious

Acharyya, R. (2017, March 7). 7 Self-Management Skills every Manager should have. Careerizma. https://www.careerizma.com/blog/self-management-skills/

Adaptability Skills: Definition and Examples | Indeed.com. (2021, July 7). Www.indeed.com. https://www.indeed.com/career-advice/career-development/adaptability-skills

Alpert, J. (2015, November 3). 7 Tips for Saying No Effectively. Inc.com. https://www.inc.com/jonathan-alpert/7-ways-to-say-no-to-someone-and-not-feel-bad-about-it.html

Amin, H. (2019, December 3). How to make accountability a core part of your workplace culture. Hypercontext. https://hypercontext.com/blog/management-skills/create-culture-accountability-workplace

Autenrieth, N. (n.d.). 10 Steps to Setting and Achieving Goals at Work. TopResume. https://in.topresume.com/career-advice/10-steps-to-setting-and-reaching-goals-at-work

Bailey, S. (2019). 4 tips for being more flexible and adaptable. Bizjournals.com. https://www.bizjournals.com/bizjournals/how-to/growth-strategies/2014/03/4-tips-for-being-more-flexible-and-adaptable.html

Cyprus, J. (2016, January 2). 7 Ways to Relieve Stress as a Manager. Psych Central. https://psychcentral.com/blog/7-ways-to-relieve-stress-as-a-manager#3

Daum, K. (2015, May 15). 8 Habits of Highly Accountable People. Inc.com; Inc. https://www.inc.com/kevin-daum/8-habits-of-highly-accountable-people.html

How New Managers Can Become More Confident [12 Great Tips]. (2018, October 16). The 6Q Blog. https://inside.6q.io/managers-become-more-confident/

Kos, B. (2020, December 16). How to become a highly organized manager: The best time management tips | Spica International. Www.spica.com. https://www.spica.com/blog/how-to-become-an-organized-manager

Managing your workload: how to manage your free time: Unifrog Blog. (n.d.). Www.unifrog.org. https://www.unifrog.org/know-how/managing-your-workload-how-to-manage-your-free-time

McD, K. (2020, February 9). 9 Ways to Build Meaningful Relationships that Matter. Myquestionlife.com. https://myquestionlife.com/build-meaningful-relationships/

Oliveira, W. (2018, August 30). 10 Expert Productivity Tips for Business Managers. HEFLO BPM. https://www.heflo.com/blog/productivity/productivity-tips-for-managers/

Perry, E. (2022, February 28). 7 Steps of the Decision-Making Process in Management. Www.betterup.com. https://www.betterup.com/blog/decision-making-process-in-management

Porteous, C. (2019, September 2). 12 Effective Time Management Skills for Managers. Lifehack. https://www.lifehack.org/844532/time-management-skills-for-managers

Problem Solving Skills That Managers Need To Have. (2019, October 11). Vantage Circle HR Blog. https://blog.vantagecircle.com/problem-solving-skills/

Rebecca. (2020, April 7). 10 Simple Ways to Set Priorities in Life. Minimalism Made Simple. https://www.minimalismmadesimple.com/home/priorities-in-life/

Self-Management Skills: Definition and Examples. (2021, December 9). Indeed, Career Guide. https://in.indeed.com/career-advice/career-development/self-management

Sestric, L. (2017, December 20). 15 Tips To Create Meaningful Relationships at Work. GOBankingRates. https://www.gobankingrates.com/money/jobs/building-relationships-at-work/

Ten Tips on Managing Change. (2010, July 1). AllBusiness.com. https://www.allbusiness.com/ten-tips-on-managing-change-11336-1.html

The Self-Care Guide for Managers | Calm for Business. (n.d.). Business.calm.com. https://business.calm.com/resources/blog/self-care-guide-for-managers

The Importance of Self-Management Skills | Glassdoor. (2021, June 29). Glassdoor Blog. https://www.glassdoor.com/blog/guide/self-management/

Wolf, J. (2021, October 25). 10 tips to improve your work-life balance | BetterUp. Www.betterup.com. https://www.betterup.com/blog/work-life-balanc

ABOUT THE AUTHOR

M. J. Pontus is an experienced manager also an entrepreneur with a wealth of knowledge and expertise in the hospitality industry. With over 15 years of experience in the field, she has held management positions at renowned companies in London, where she has made a lasting impact on her exceptional performance.

Besides her management skills, she is also an avid writer. Her first book, "Management for Beginners", offers her management knowledge to help both novice and experiences managers become effective leaders in various businesses. "Manage You!" is her second book in a management series. She is passionate about helping people succeed in their careers, particularly in the corporate world.

According to M. J., becoming an excellent manager is not something that happens overnight, but rather a long and difficult journey that involves working with others. In her books, she pays tribute to the teams she has worked with and her mentors, who have helped shaped her management skills. More books from M. J., including those on management topics, are in the works.

SHARE YOUR THOUGHTS

I hope you enjoyed the book. I would love for you to share your thoughts about it:

https://bit.ly/ManageYou

Or you can connect with me directly via:

- My website   https://www.mjpontus.com
- Facebook   https://www.facebook.com/mjpontus
- Instagram   https://www.instagram.com/mjpontus

MORE BOOKS FROM M.J. PONTUS

Are you ready to become a successful manager? This book is the perfect guide for aspiring and newly appointed managers like you!

In this book, you'll learn how to select the right management style, build trust with your team, and smoothly transition into your new role. You'll also learn how to improve our organisational culture, communicate effectively, and become a great coach for your team. Plus, you'll get some helpful advice on how to cope with the stress of being a manager.

Get your copy of Management For Beginners,

and start mastering the skills you need to succeed as a manager!

www.ingramcontent.com/pod-product-compliance
Lightning Source LLC
Chambersburg PA
CBHW041137110526
44590CB00027B/4046